# ULTIMATE PLAYBOOK for High Performing SALES TEAMS

**RANDALL GRIZZLE · DEBORAH BURRIS**

www.CloserSecrets.com

Copyright © 2021 Deborah Burris and Randall Grizzle

All rights reserved.

No part of this book may be reproduced in any form or by any electronic or mechanical means, including information storage and retrieval systems, without the express written permission from the authors, except for the use of brief quotations in a book review.

Cover and Images by Vince Palko/Ad Toons

# Praise for
# Closer Secrets Ultimate Playbook for High Performing Sales Teams

I met Randall years ago when he was working as a closer with Russel Brunson at ClickFunnels. As I was listening to Randall's sales call, I was so intrigued by how the conversation went completely opposite than I thought. Normally on sales calls, you hear the pitch and then decide. Randall did the opposite, he allowed me to express my concerns and walked me through them, gave me advice (not knowing if I'd join or not) and by the end, I was ready to join.

I wondered how he was able to do that. He created an environment for me of service vs how so many others do it in making it feel so salesy and completely unheard.

A few years later, I'd grown a great following that was asking for more of my time and my team and we created a product that I knew would change lives. I recalled how Randall made me feel in the sales call and wondered if he could help train me and my team.

I reached out and this was exactly what he was doing. Training others to take the slime out of higher ticket item sales and lead with service as he'd done in my sales call. I immediately signed up and he set me up with Deborah who was basically the project manager/integrator (and now BFF) on rolling this out perfectly. She set up a seamless workflow, trained my team, and went over and beyond by referring top talent that has been an absolute blessing to my business. One of our favorite parts ever was working with Deborah. She continues to go above and beyond.

Because we learned to serve vs 'sell', smooth out the processes to get calls, applications forms in place, and get the results for our clients, we sell out of our program each time we put it out to the market.

I had plenty of questions along the way and they helped me navigate some tricky waters and new territory as they've had years of experience with this process.

-Alison J Prince, CEO/Founder, Alison J Prince

Working with the Closer Secrets team has been a game-changer for me. As a marketer, the hardest part of every business is always to turn the prospecting leads into customers. Randall's approach to sales has been proven to be extremely effective. Not only is it customizable and fits all industries, but it's also very unique and efficient. I highly recommend working with the Closer Secrets team.

-Jason Burlin, CEO/Founder, Burlin Digital

Closer Secrets is a great resource of credible, skilled and highly valuable insights that produce some of the industries top closers.

-Jeremy Haynes, CEO/Founder, Megalodon Marketing

"I've had the pleasure of working with Deborah Burris for some time, and as a sales leader in my own company have watched her help multiple teams scale to 10x their original size while still retaining the culture that made them successful in the first place. She has done this through a combination of codifying processes, helping to implement great toolsets, and helping her clients put the appropriate resources behind the parts of their business that will make them most successful. WIth all the "sales gurus" out there, it has been refreshing to deal with someone who deeply cares about her clients and utilizes time-tested, demonstrable strategies to truly help them grow."

-David Gable, Director of Growth, Kixie

Randall, Deborah, Val, and the team at Closer Secrets are World-Class. They don't mess around, and they basically take everything off your plate when it comes to running a successful sales organization. They recruit the best talent, they organize that talent, they motivate that talent, and they track and scoreboard all the numbers to hold everyone accountable. They aren't the cheapest & they don't work with everyone but they are incredible to work with and we have been blessed to meet and work with them for a long time now.

-Kale Abrahamson, CEO, Nine University

When I started with closer secrets I was selling all my own deals . I still hadn't built a sales team or sold 7 figures online . Randall taught me the art of high ticket . Instantly I raised the prices of my products and increased profit . He also referred me to some of the best salespeople that I've ever worked with . They went on to build a sales team that took my business to 3 million in sales in 12 months . In one day I closed 500k in business and The Closer Secret team helped with the entire thing . Randall has always given my business individual care and has kept my best interest in every deal . He is the definition of a great salesman . He delivers and what he says he's going to do and is a man of high character. If you want to master high ticket and scale your business 3x then Randall is the guy you need on your team.

-Lee Haight, Owner, Sky Diamond's & RRCA

In my 2 decade career as a personal growth and development instructor I have had many chances to work with and support some amazing organizations. When I book other professionals to speak from my stages or be an expert contributor to speak on specific high level skill sets I research and get the best. Randall is one of the most grounded and proficient high ticket sales experts there is in my opinion. From the stage or any other form he chooses to pass along his wisdom and insights he is the very best at transferring his vast knowledge into true tangible and leverageable results! His heart and passion infused leadership mixed with the talents of Deborah Burris is a recipe for success. She is a master technician at providing insights and tools on efficiencies for the closer and their clients. I have the utmost respect for her as a person and as the person who can take great to extraordinary and beyond.

To have them sharing their combined knowledge of setting up win-win scenarios and real life hard hitting knowledge is a powerful combination! I can not speak highly enough of the talents and minds that have collaborated to give over the top value to any reader of this book. In an industry where you either sink or swim this is a must have compilation of years and years of high producing experience. I honor anyone who cares enough about their results to take on the best of the tools available to set themselves up for success, congratulations on being one of those amazing individuals.

-Todd L. Campbell, CEO, T.C.C., Inc.

The way that Randall teaches how to sell is of the utmost of integrity, which is important to me because I am a practicing attorney. I like for people to have an amazing experience. I want them to be thrilled with the decision they have made and that is the process that Randall teaches. If you are on the fence about whether or not to work with Randall Grizzle, let me tell you something: you have to do it. This guy is the best of the best. I have seen other people out there; they don't even hold a candle to the knowledge and the level of integrity that Randall brings to the table. If you can learn his secret sauce, his system, your business is going to change. I know mine has.

-Natasha Hazlett, CEO, Fast Forward Marketing

Closer Secrets – Randall and Valerie Grizzle, Deborah Burris and the rest of their team are some of the best in the world at scaling, growing, managing and running a high performing sales team. When we brought them into our business we were in a bit of a slump, and over the past year the sales team they've managed has called on 10's of thousands of leads, generated millions of dollars, and all the while doing it the RIGHT way – no outlandish claims, no pushy sales tactics – simply working with the prospects to figure out what was the best for that person. They run our sales team – and I'm going to be reading this book to figure out how they did it – because they delivered results well above my expectations.

-Taylor Hiott, Nine University

To business owners who create value that provides real opportunity for change.

To sales professionals who represent with truth and integrity.

"Let your light so shine before men, that they may see your good works, and glorify your Father which is in heaven."

Matthew 5:16

# Contents

| | |
|---|---|
| Forward | xv |
| Introduction | xix |

## The Big Picture — 1

| | |
|---|---|
| Chapter 1: Position to Win | 3 |
|     Straight Line to Success | 3 |
|     Purpose, Mission, Value Statements | 4 |
|     Create Clarity and Motivation | 6 |
| Chapter 2: Crafting an Intentional Culture | 9 |
|     Embrace the Pulse | 9 |
|     Prepare Yourself to Lead | 13 |
|     Winning T.E.A.M Elements | 14 |

## The Playbook — 21

| | |
|---|---|
| Chapter 3: From the Clubhouse to the Field | 25 |
|     Attracting Sales Superstars | 25 |
|     Sales Management Philosophy and Expectations | 27 |
|     Business Owner's Why | 27 |
|     Media Links | 28 |
| Chapter 4: Clarity on the Funnel and Offer | 31 |
|     Funnel Flow | 31 |
|     Lead Types | 32 |
|     Learning Resources | 34 |
|     Offer Stack | 34 |
|     Offer Descriptions | 35 |
| Chapter 5: Intentional Sales Process | 39 |
|     Pre-Call | 39 |
|     Sales Methodologies | 40 |

| | |
|---|---|
| Post Call | 41 |
| Payment Processing Protocols | 42 |
| Enrollment | 43 |
| Customer Success | 43 |
| **Chapter 6: Element of a Winning Script** | **47** |
| Winning Script Framework | 49 |
| Probe | 50 |
| Blast | 50 |
| Commitments | 51 |
| Close | 52 |
| Onboarding | 53 |
| **Chapter 7: Effective Call Execution** | **55** |
| Situational Role Play | 55 |
| Embrace Your Native Genius | 57 |
| Review Recordings | 59 |
| Prepare for Common Objections | 61 |
| Effective Visual Pitch Techniques | 63 |
| Compliance | 65 |
| **Chapter 8: Tools & Techniques for Optimal Performance** | **69** |
| Company Branded Email | 70 |
| Appointment Scheduling Platform | 70 |
| Customer Relationship Management (CRM) | 71 |
| Phone System | 72 |
| Team Communication | 73 |
| Integration: Zapier | 74 |
| User and Security Protocols | 75 |
| **Chapter 9: Effective Sales Meetings & Reviews** | **77** |
| Know Your Numbers | 77 |
| Express Gratitude | 79 |
| Encourage Sharing | 81 |
| Provide Leadership Opportunity | 81 |

| | |
|---|---|
| Encourage Business Owner Interaction | 81 |
| Effective Closer Performance Reviews | 82 |
| **Chapter 10: F.O.C.U.S. Resources** | **85** |
| Frequently Occurring Customer and User Situations (F.O.C.U.S.) | 85 |
| Closer Support | 85 |
| Customer Support | 86 |
| **Chapter 11: Winning Based on Fact Not Emotion** | **89** |
| Sustainable Success is in the Numbers | 89 |
| Resolving Leads | 91 |
| Geographic Ad Spend ROI | 94 |
| Understanding your Numbers | 95 |
| Profitability by Closer | 96 |
| **Chapter 12: Motivating Compensation Models** | **99** |
| Spiffs | 99 |
| Static | 100 |
| Sliding Scale | 100 |
| Payday: How and When | 101 |
| **Conclusion** | **103** |
| **Map** | **108** |
| **Author Bios** | **110** |

# Forward

They say evolution is the key to success in business.

I would say that in the phone sales industry this is probably truer than almost any other industry on the planet. When I was a young kid I watched the show Boiler Room and was fascinated with how a sales floor operated. You've probably got a vision in your head of a bunch of people in one big room screaming and hollering every time a sale is made right?

That's exactly how sales floors were run when I first started in this industry over a decade ago, I'll never forget walking into a room with 200 or more people all on the phones selling products related to my brand.

The energy in that room was insane!

Fast-forward to today, almost 10 years later, and the industry has evolved as more and more services become available online.

Today many sales teams are simply a collection of closers working from home.

No big rooms.

No insane energy.

To be honest this is a great evolution for the industry because it allows companies to hire the best closers regardless of their geographic location. However, with this evolution to the industry came many problems and obstacles that did not exist when everyone was in one big room.

How do you create energy on your sales team?

How do you monitor their performance and call time?

How do you motivate people who are likely sitting at home, to be on the phones as much as humanly possible?

It's for these reasons that most sales floors, even when they were not remote, failed within the first year or two of opening.

I've seen the industry change so much since my first sales team 10 years ago and the one thing I know you must have in order to survive and thrive are the right people, right systems and right processes in place to ensure long term success.

In 2019 I decided I wanted to ramp back up my phone sales and I immediately realized it just wasn't as easy as it was when I first started in this industry.

How would I handle all these new obstacles?

Luckily for me I found Closer Secrets and really bought in to what they teach and their process.

Randall and Deborah have developed a very unique system that does the Following:

1. Find good quality closers – notice I didn't say "hustlers" or "grinders" I said good QUALITY closers. This is so important because when people are selling on your brand they are representing YOU. Never sacrifice quality just for bigger sales numbers, that's the short game.

2. Implement efficient systems – like I said earlier managing your leads is one of the key metrics for success, but how do you do that when everyone is scattered all over the world? The unique system that Closer Secrets has in place allows you to not only manage your leads, but also optimize the ROI you can generate from each lead generated.

3. Train and Motivate – it's important to keep your sales people motivated each and every day. If you've run a sales team in the past you know there are periods of ups and and downs throughout the year. It's how your team reacts during the "down times" that truly determines your success. The training that Closer Secrets provides on a weekly basis keeps your

team dialed in and ready for success.

Through their unique process and training we've been able to scale our team and sales to numbers we've not had in over a decade.

The most important thing to me when it comes to phone sales is to always operate with truth and integrity, which is something both Randall and Deborah consistently teach and instill in everyone who goes through their program or works with their Closer Secrets agency.

Ultimately we live in a world where that old school telephone is still one of the most powerful selling devices we can access, but to maximize it's effects on your business you need a sales team that properly trained and operating the Closer Secrets way.

In this book you're going to learn how that's done, which can completely transform your business so that you're making more sales, helping more people and operating at your peak level of performance.

- Anthony Morrison

# Introduction

We live in a world of systems, processes and automation, which allow us to do more with less, remove human error from the equation and spend more time doing things we truly enjoy.

Business owners around the globe use these technologies to target and communicate a consistent message to an audience, qualify prospects, and in some cases close a sale without ever having any human interaction.

With all of this "automation" running, why are top sales people aggressively recruited, and why are sales departments the most highly paid within most organizations?

The answer is simple: while business decisions are best made using data and logic, sales are best made with reflection and emotion. No matter how amazing a system is, it will never be able to replace the human connection.

Today, sales people are called many things, such as: High Ticket Closers, Strategy Advisors and Enrollment Coaches. Regardless of their title, the highest performers in the "sales industry" never focus on "selling." The best in this industry focus on being the best at helping others gain clarity on the change they seek, why that change is necessary, and how they can help them get there.

This book is not about slick tactics to induce your sales team to perform, or your prospects to purchase your offer. If that is what you are looking for, go ahead and stop here.

This book is about getting clear about the change you and your offer bring to the world. It is about finding the perfect balance of automation and human interaction to enable you to maximize opportunity. It is about making intelligent business decisions based on data, not emotion. It is about having the right systems and processes in place, to ensure your sales team comes from a place of truth with each customer interaction. It is about instilling confidence along every step of the customer journey. It is about changing the traditional sales process, which can be deceitful and manipulative. It is about differentiation by providing real opportunity that attracts the right customers, the right closers, and crushes the competition. Ultimately, it is about coming from a place of truth and transparency.

# The Big Picture

"I need a closer!" These are the most common four words out of the mouth of businesses that reach out to Closer Secrets. But is this really what they need to get their offer off the ground or scale their business to the next level?

The answer is yes and no. Yes, because ultimately, a business with a high ticket offer will need closers to monetize it. No, because without an intentional game plan in place, a closer can often unintentionally sabotage a winning offer before it gets a fair shot at success.

Putting an offer together and throwing a couple of closers on the phone to see how much they can sell is risky. You could have created the most profitable offer with the highest demand and most customer value seen in a decade, but if your sales process is not set up right, the closers can be what torpedoes the offer, instead of launching it to exceed expectations.

In this book, you will learn how having a Playbook for your sales team can maximize every dollar you are spending on traffic and fulfillment, while maximizing the efficiency of your sales team. Having a game plan in place exponentially increases your probability of success. No winning team starts the game with the opening kick off, first at-bat, or opening tip-off without a solid game plan in place, and neither should you.

# Chapter 1: Position to Win

*"Coming together is a beginning, staying together is progress, and working together is success.*

-Henry Ford

## Straight Line to Success

In elementary school we all learn that the shortest distance between two points is a straight line. Why then, do so many companies set their organizational goals out of alignment with their sales goals? Most of the time, this misalignment is not intentional, rather a common trap of each department operating in a vacuum. This is because the leadership in the company is not taking the time to define the business with clarity and intention. Any friction between the company goals and it's sales team goals slows performance.

Think of your offer or company as your dream car. You have thought about it and saved for it (sometimes for years) before you are to the point of having everything together to hit the world highway. Now the car needs gas. Sales are the fuel that keeps your offer and your company alive. Sales are what allow you to have the resources to innovate and expand continually. The best fuel, combined with the straightest map, results in optimal performance and crossing the finish line of your goals in record time.

Every winner of the Indy 500 used high octane fuel and had a highly seasoned pit crew. Do you think they just show up the day of the race and hope for the best? No, of course not. They spend the days and weeks before the race mapping the course, studyingthe track, working on strategy, timing and preparing their pits and their crew. They prep for every scenario possible, so when race day comes there are few to no surprises. So when you are looking to map your course and hire your pit crew, ask yourself the following questions:

- What level of salesperson does your organization attract?
- Does your sales management team enable maximum performance?
- Is the path you have laid for your organization straight, or does it have some curves that are confusing to navigate, friction that slows progress?
- How do you align sales with your overall company goals?

## Purpose, Mission, Value Statements

A critical element to building an effective offer is to get clear on the purpose, mission, and value statements behind your business. Clarity is key and it all starts with you. Laying a sturdy foundation for your business is critical to ensuring a strong and stable structure from which to build upon. Taking the time to create these statements will help you solidify a foundation and build a business that is true to its core values. As a company you should take the time to map out the cornerstones. It seems rudimentary, but you might be surprised how many people just want to start a business and not take the time to sit down and write out the discipline for their business. Business purpose, missions statements and the value you bring to the consumer, are a few examples. If you don't know who you are as a company (what your values and purpose are) how is anyone going to be able to sell for you? These help ensure your messaging is clear and consistently attracts the right kind of customer and that your sales team is accurately communicating that message.

## Business purpose

The purpose of your business relates to what it does to help your ideal customer. Why does your company exist? You should be able to fine tune your business purpose down to a single sentence, maybe two. It can also be known as your catch phrase for your business. Think about what problems you **want** to solve for your clients on a large scale. This is the purpose for your business. Then narrow this down to the ones you **can** solve. Finally, ensure these align with what your ideal clients want and need. The sentence should be broad in scope, but specific to the value you provide for the customer. This is the reason for the existence of your company.

## Your mission

Your mission refers to what your business is trying to achieve for the owners (and shareholders, if any). At first glance, it may seem selfish to think this way. But in reality, it's a necessary and practical component of any business and its funnels. It is meant to provide a focus for your team. You need to be clear on exactly what your end goal is, so you can ensure your marketing is helping you reach it, rather than taking you further from it.

For example, perhaps you have a number in mind for how much you'd like to profit in the next 12-month period. This can help you figure out how many new customers you need to bring on board with your funnel.

You likely also have some idea of what your day-to-day life will look like during this process. For example, is working 60-hour weeks to attain this goal faster acceptable to you? Or do you only have 40 hours a week to devote to this goal?

The answers to these questions will help you determine how best to market your high ticket offer. It may even cause you to modify your offer in a way that allows you to more easily stay true to your mission.

### Value statements

These help you stay true to who you are and what you believe in. Your company's value statement will describe the intended culture you wish to display. This statement will set core principles and directions for the company and it's employees or contractors. In essence, what you will and won't put up with in the confines of your business. Here is a list of what carefully crafted value statements can do for your company:

- set the tone for the expected behavior of all company staff, including you as the owner
- ensure staff conducts themselves with integrity
- maintain a company culture that's in keeping with your business's purpose and overall mission
- guide your decision-making process
- help to prioritize what to focus on

Take the time to figure out your company values — it's a task you only have to do once, and will provide you with increased clarity in all future decisions you make regarding your business. Remember, if your business sets and stays firmly in its values, it will make every other decision in the company easier.

Take the time to set your values in your business. As your company grows it will be important to have your values articulated and written down so they can be shared. These values will help to ensure that the company is working toward the same common goal and share the bigger purpose.

## Create Clarity and Motivation

When you clearly articulate the essential concepts for your business, it becomes exponentially more comfortable to move forward. They help make the best course of action evident since only the right choices will align with your purpose, mission, and value statements.

A clear purpose helps motivate your sales team since they know what their primary objective will be. It will eliminate gray areas and help team members move into action because the vision of the company is clear, and aligned. Ask yourself, if I were to ask a handful of employees to describe the organization, would their answers be consistent, or all over the board? If your team can't name the values that drive your company, how are they to work towards them?

Your mission helps keep you as a business owner laser focused on the right things. Ensuring everyone is on board with your company's value statements means you'll have a sales process and business that is in alignment.

# Chapter 2: Crafting an Intentional Culture

*"The strength of a team is each individual member. The strength of each member is the team."*

-Phil Jackson

## Embrace the Pulse

When building your business you are not just trying to solve problems and get revenue. You are creating a culture. Your business will create a multitude of habits, beliefs and procedures for a variety of people that are touched by your company. It's the natural process of life, the gathering of people who work together. This culture should be created with intent. Your purpose, mission and values all play a role in the development of this culture. So what would you like your team to say about your company? Once you set your purpose and values, what can the leadership do to ensure the concepts are being portrayed in the company? How do you enhance the quality of the business while also increasing the overall well-being of the individual in the day to day operations?

The first step to building a high performing sales team is to see each team member as an individual. See them as people. This may sound elementary and perhaps even goofy at first, but it is critical to the success of your team. The sales team is not just the workhorse to sell your product or service. If you stop for just a moment to think about it, most organizations look at sales team members not as people but as objects. The customer, many times, sees them as someone just trying to get money from them. The boss sees them as an overpaid necessity. Both of those scenarios lead to a position of feeling undervalued as a person. Do you remember seeing that disgruntled employee on top of the sales board? Me neither.

Keeping the morale of a sales team high is easier than a lot of people think. The "ego" that most people don't like when they think of a stereotypical salesperson is the same "ego" that is needed to keep them as high performing members of your team.

So what's the secret to promoting morale and keeping everyone happy? Recognition. A little recognition goes a long way in the sales world.

## Chapter 2: Crafting an Intentional Culture

*Early on in my professional career, the Vice President of Sales for the major pharmaceutical company I worked with recognized me at an award ceremony for being #1 out of 88 sales team members in my division. He then proceeded to give a speech referring to the sales division as revenue-producing units (RPU's) The silver cup I received awarding my achievement was nice, but every time I look at it I think RPU! Thankfully, my direct manager, Jerry Smith saw each of us as individuals. He recognized our strengths and weaknesses and helped each of us become better. He knew what was important to us and did all he could to help us achieve our goals. While working with him I purchased my first home. I told him I was going to take a couple days off to scrape all the "popcorn" off the ceiling so the remodeling team could come and retexture the ceilings before moving onto painting, putting in new flooring etc. Not only was Jerry supportive of giving me the time off he actually showed up at my house with a bandana wrapped around his head with jeans and a t-shirt on ready to work. I couldn't believe it! Jerry was known in this primadonna industry as being the best dressed, most manicured among us! As we were wetting down the ceilings and scraping all that nastiness off the ceiling I asked him why he took the time to help me with such an undesirable job. His reply was "you are my top performer. By helping you finish this faster you can get back out there and sell more, besides I used to work construction and knew how hard this was going to be and wanted to give you a hand." Jerry seeing everyone on our team as real people made us all perform at the highest level. We simply would not accept anything but being first because we had a first class leader who cared.*     DB

Recognition will empower your team. Receiving a physical award will carry a long way. Not only is the appreciation shown, in a big way, during the presentation of the award, but it will also serve as a reminder every time the sales person catches a glimpse of the object they were presented with. This is the very reason high performing athletes have a trophy room. Human nature loves to remember the successes.

But this in no way means that it takes pomp and circumstance to make your individual team members feel important and empowered. It's often the little things, the daily things, that will be impactful on the morale of your salesperson. How are your team meetings run? Is it a talking head directing behaviors? An open conversation asking for feedback? Does your company show the team the value in their voice or experience? Increasing the engagement with your sales personnel will boost morale. The more contribution the better. After all, they are the first contact with your customers.

> *I had been working for a successful internet marketing company for a few years and the company threw a gala in honor of the company's birthday. Of course there was recognition for support staff and management, applause and a few plaques were handed out. Then for the sales team they did something different. They came up with their own version of "The Razzies" a spoof award for every sales member. Yes, they all poked a little fun at the individual, but also honored everyone as they walked up to get their plastic trophy. Management took notice of everyone on the sales floor. They paid attention to quirks and personalities and awarded each member for their uniqueness. It wasn't a huge award, but it was personal attention.*     *RG*

Know your people. Care about them as individuals. Value their differences. Encourage individuality. Embrace their strengths. Help them make their weaknesses strong. Recognize their contributions. Praise their ideas. Above all, express genuine appreciation for them individually. Do this and closers will be excited to be a part of the team, represent your brand with integrity, and want to stay with your offers for years to come.

## Chapter 2: Crafting an Intentional Culture

> *When I think of embracing the pulse with our sales teams I think of Yoda! Yoda is a favorite of mine because he embodies careful consideration and wisdom. I have team members send me Yoda memes all the time and even received a Mandalorian toy from Randall and Val for Christmas! I keep this toy in my office and it reminds me to carefully consider the totality of each situation and each individual before making decisions that affect our closers and clients.*   *DB*

## Prepare Yourself to Lead

Each of us is the sum of all our thoughts. What we allow into our daily lives is what we will portray onto others. Ever notice how your day goes when you go for that morning run? Or see a shift in your mood when you watch a devastating movie? What about the energy you bring after you watch or read a hero's story? How about transitions in mood before and after you log onto social media? The things we let into our lives, in turn, shape our energy, our mood and who we become as people. Lead from the front by guarding what you allow to enter your mind. This separates those who succeed from those who fail.

> *On my journey from employee to entrepreneur I have faced lots of opportunities to develop personally. I had been at several networking events and over the course of time had one of my new acquaintances, Anthony DeClemente, invited me to be a part of his bio-hacking experience. Now, I was aware of my health and how it wasn't where I wanted it to be. I was nervous about what I was getting myself into.*
>
> *The excursion required me to leave my family and travel to Chicago, in November, and spend a week with people I didn't know, in a town I wasn't familiar with. I was excited and nervous at the same time. I released all preconceived notions of how I thought it would go and was able to fully engage in the experience, which included 10 minutes in the brisk waters of Lake Michigan. I opened myself up to possibilities and was able to grow as a person and business leader from the experience.* —RG

It is Helmu Schmidt who said "The biggest room in the world is the room for improvement." Successful entrepreneurs and closers set aside time daily for self improvement. This can be taking the time to meditate, listen to audiobooks, podcasts, read uplifting content, and do things they love with people they love.

Some of our best ideas come when we are not "working". After all, why work...if you don't play?

## Winning T.E.A.M Elements

Every great achievement is the result of a team effort. Whether you are an entrepreneur traveling the world, a closer working from a home office, or a sales manager leading a team, there are certain key elements that need to be in place to produce the maximum beneficial outcome for everyone.

These key elements are simply communicated using T.E.A.M. as an acronym:

## Chapter 2: Crafting an Intentional Culture

T = Transparency
E = Engagement
A = Accountability
M = Mindset

### Transparency

One of our favorite quotes from Steven R. Covey is "Begin with End in Mind." This statement seems sensible and simple, however, it is surprising how often we see confusion within organizations because they fail to communicate.

As a business owner it is in your best interest to share your vision for the company with everyone in your organization. Breaking down your expectations and goals into daily, weekly, monthly, quarterly and yearly expectations is powerful. It gives your team clarity on what is expected and allows them to digest how each of these benchmarks, when met, will benefit them.

A smart closer will be proactive in communicating their expectations when joining a sales team and be very open about the results they expect to achieve based on the offer they are selling. They will also ask questions if they don't understand something about the offer, processes, or systems used. Providing clear and timely notice of call availability, vacations and other needs is key to doing your part as a TEAM member.

### Engagement

Diligently working toward the goals you set and shared as part of Transparency is great. But if you are doing it in a vacuum, things could be better.

Leaders of the sales team that are serious about maximizing opportunity, take the time to have regular interactions with the business owners and their closers. This can be done in various ways depending on the type of organization you have. The common denominator for successful companies is they are *intentional* about their engagement. Having standing, regularly scheduled appointments on your calendar with key individuals and departments is a must. Providing less formal opportunities to engage, such as team lunches, management retreats, and golf outings, are also effective ways to connect and take the pulse of your organization.

In an increasingly remote environment, it is critical to know your people. Not being in a brick-and-mortar building leads to another layer of disconnect. There is more opportunity for members to feel lost in the company. All too often we notice the creator of the company is too busy being an influencer and not a leader. They are not taking the time to be a part of the culture they are creating. Honestly, it is as simple as taking the time once a month, or even quarter to get on a sales team meeting and check in with everyone. It might only take five minutes out of your day, but would mean a great deal to those you are talking to. Take the time to notice and comment when you see something happening, even if it is not work-related.

## Accountability

Whether you are watching the number on the scale go down when trying to lean out or watching your numbers go up as you take the lead on the sales board, accountability always improves results. Math trumps emotion when it comes to growing a successful business. Numbers reveal, without bias, what is effective and what is ineffective.

Savvy entrepreneurs will know their numbers. Numbers will be a significant factor in all critical business decisions. Each arm of an organization should have clearly defined key performance indicators (KPI's), which are reported on a regularly scheduled basis. There are many KPI's in each department. Here are the most critical KPI's for key departments within a sales organization:

- Sales:

    Dollar per lead (DPL). This is the total dollar amount collected divided by the number of completed calls.

- Marketing

    Cost per lead (CPL) This is the total dollar amount spent driving traffic divided by the number of leads generated.

## Chapter 2: Crafting an Intentional Culture

- Customer Success:

    Net promoter Score (NPS) This is the number of promoters minus the total number of detractors divided by the total number of respondents times 100. The Net Promoter Score is considered to be the standard measure across industries for customer satisfaction, loyalty, and likelihood your customers will refer others.

Closers thrive on competition. Most sales teams are now virtual. Having a mechanism in place to display a virtual sales board in real-time is highly effective. There are many ways to make this information available, depending on the systems you have in place. Closer Secret's Lead Tracker is a highly effective solution (more on this in Chapter 9).

### Mindset

Closers at times, have the mindset of keeping key learnings in their pocket to maintain a competitive advantage. The truth is, the best Closers are TEAM players. They openly share with other team members what is working and not working so everyone can benefit.

Good closers become great closers when transparency is a part of their mindset. Communicating things that were effective and things that were ineffective, in the spirit of mutual respect and a desire to help everyone be more successful, is the mark of an excellent closer.

> *Early on in my sales career I completed the Dale Carnegie training course. Our class met in person for months. Each week we would be given an assignment based on the topic we were studying about human behavior. When we gathered together the following week it was fascinating to hear everyone's real world experiences. Those that shared their experiences with a mindset of learning together from the things they implemented that worked and didn't work got the most out of the experience. It is the same way with the closers we manage on our teams. The best among them share their successes and failures so that the entire team can benefit. These are without exception the members of the team that make the most money and rise up to become respected leaders.* —*DB*

# The Playbook

*"The only thing worse than training your employees and having them leave is not training them and having them stay."*

-Henry Ford

After you've aligned your overall business goals with your sales goals and set your entire organization in a clearly defined straight line to success, it's time to focus on the game plan that will help your team be prepared and convert as many prospects into customers as possible. To maximize results, it's vital that you have a well thought out strategy, which we call the "Playbook".

You need to be clear on exactly what your offer is, how you will present it to your leads, what your goals are, and how you're going to measure the success of your strategy.

Here are some things you should think about during this process (all of which will be covered in detail later):

- How to identify the right people for your sales team
- How to navigate the transition from marketing to selling
- Creating an intentional sales process

- Importance of a solid script and monitoring calls for compliance
- Providing the tools your sales team needs to succeed
- Effective management of your sales team
- Empowering your sales team to serve customers
- Creating a motivating compensation model for closers

# Chapter 3: From the Clubhouse to the Field

*"Perfection is not attainable. But if we chase perfection, we can catch excellence."*

-Vince Lombardi

## Attracting Sales Superstars

Anyone on your company's team is a direct reflection of you and your brand. It is important to thoroughly vet out each closer to ensure they are not only competent, but also a culture fit for the offer and the sales team.

### Interview Process

Since the pool of closers is literally unlimited by geographical location, this is best accomplished by having the prospective closer schedule a Zoom call with sales management. If the prospective closer does not follow up on this simple step they are disqualified. Persistence, desire, and follow through are hallmarks of any great closer.

During the video interview some important questions to ask are:

- What do you know about the company and this offer?
- What attracted you to the influencer?
- What is your sales experience?

- How have you performed on other offers?
- Why did you choose High Ticket closing as a career?
- What strengths can you bring to the team?
- What weaknesses can this team help you make strong?
- What is your understanding of call compliance?
- What is your availability?
- Will you be dedicated 100% to this opportunity?
- What is your annual income goal?
- What days of the week are you available?
- What is your "Why"?

It is recommended to have a second interview connecting the prospective closer with a member of the sales team. If the sales team has a team leader who also closes on the team it is recommended the second interview be with the team leader. The second interview serves two purposes:

1. It allows the prospective closer to ask questions to a person actively selling on the team. This is often a much less intimidating environment to ask questions and get a true feel for the offer's pitch.
2. It also lets the team leader evaluate if this is someone they feel would be a good addition to the team. It is good to bring on new closers that bring unique, yet complimentary flavor to the team so it can consistently progress.

## Independent Contractors & Documents

Closers are almost always brought on as independent contractors. They are usually contracted with a sales management team like Closer Secrets. In certain situations they can also be contracted by the organization. Factors that determine which of these scenarios is best, include the size of the team, the size of the organization, the size of the payroll, and the long term vision for the sales department.

In either scenario, each independent contractor should sign the following documents before any confidential information is shared or they are allowed to take any calls:

## Chapter 3: From the Clubhouse to the Field

- Independent Contractor Agreement: The purpose of this agreement is to clearly define the closer's independent contractor status. Typically it states the commission structure, dates payments will be processed, amount of reserve withheld if any, timeline for potential clawbacks, and a confidentiality clause.
- Direct Deposit: Direct deposit information can be associated with the closer's individual banking information or with their legal entity's banking information. More and more closers are setting up their own Limited Liability Companies (LLC's) so they can operate and be taxed as a company.
- Tax Forms: For US Residents it is required to have a W9 tax form on file which has the necessary information to file a 1099-Misc form at the end of each year for the closer as an individual using their social security number or the closer's legal entity using a registered EIN number. For Non-US residents a W-8BEN form is required.

## Sales Management Philosophy and Expectations

Many sales professionals look for opportunities with Closer Secrets because they are known as a sales management organization with integrity. Whether you are running your sales operations internally or hiring an external sales management team, it is critical they are in alignment with the organization's purpose, mission and values. It is helpful for the sales management team to record a video on their philosophy and expectations for the team. This can be put at the top of the team Playbook, so the entire team knows what is expected and all are on the same page.

## Business Owner's Why

Every successful business owner has a story of how their offer came into existence. It is extremely powerful to have the sales team hear the story directly from the business owner. When the closers understand the "Why" of the business owner, it becomes easier to communicate the value of the offer. Connect the dots on an emotional level for your closer and they will be able to transfer that energy over to their sales calls. The passion of the business owner and their desire to share their vehicle of success with others is powerful. With the business owner's permission we recommend recording this and putting it at the beginning of the playbook so subsequent closers can watch, listen and benefit from the "Why!"

## Media Links

We exist in a high paced world of social media; use it to your advantage. In order for closers to become familiar with the brand and style of an organization, it is helpful to provide them a list of media links. Access to private groups and training should be reserved until a closer has completed their training. Certain access could be withheld until they pass certain benchmarks. Possible media links include, but are not limited to:

- Facebook
- Instagram
- Tik Tok
- YouTube
- Twitter
- Podcasts
- Forums
- LiveWebinars

# Chapter 4: Clarity on the Funnel and Offer

*"Sales is an outcome, not a goal. It's a function of doing numerous things right, starting from the moment you target that potential prospect until you finalize the deal."*

-Jill Konrath

## Funnel Flow

One of the biggest disconnects we see in the industry is a lack of context. It is not uncommon for closers to be told what the offer is, have their calendars turned on and start taking booked calls without having an understanding of what that prospect experienced prior to booking a call.

To make a seamless transition from marketing to sales it is critical for closers to go through the funnel so they have the proper context when they get on the call with the prospect. If there are multiple funnels the sales team should be intimately aware of each of them.

Funnel elements to make accessible to your sales team could include:

- Optin Page
- Webinar Replay
- VSL Page (Video Sales Letter)
- Book a Call VSL Page

- Tripwire Offers
- OTO Page (One Time Offer)
- Thank you Page
- Purchase Thank You Page
- Cancel/Reschedule Redirect Page
- Application Page
- Application Confirmation Email

## Lead Types

If you have multiple lead types coming from various sources, it is helpful to have a written description of each one. This enables the closer to seamlessly grab the baton from marketing, and keep the momentum guiding the prospect to a buying decision. Common lead types include:

- Application Lead
- Event Lead
- Buyer Lead
- Outbound Lead

### Application Leads

This lead typically watches a VSL or Webinar and is then given a chance to schedule a "strategy session" after filling out an application whose purpose is to qualify them for the opportunity. The questions can be captured using Typeform, WuFoo, or a customized booking page in a scheduling platform like Once Hub. Application questions may include:

- What specifically attracted you to this opportunity?
- What is your current monthly income?
- What do you feel is the biggest obstacle preventing you from achieving your income goals?
- On a scale from 1 to 10 how committed are you?
- What makes you different from other applicants and why

## Chapter 4: Clarity on the Funnel and Offer

should we choose to work with you?
- If this opportunity makes sense for you, how soon can you get started?

### Event Leads

As the name implies, these leads are generated through events. Traditionally the majority of these events have been held live and in person. However, companies and influencers are holding more virtual events.

A hallmark of event leads is urgency. Prospects have usually spent a considerable amount of time finding out about the opportunity and getting to know the people they will be working with. This intimacy gives the influencer or company the ability to leverage the element of exclusivity and scarcity. In most cases a decision and purchase must be made before the close of the event and special bonuses are often given for those that are the first to take action.

Post event follow up will include fulfillment for those that purchased, and outbound calls to attendees that did not purchase to downsell them another offer.

### Buyer Leads

Buyer leads come through the funnel and purchase a tripwire or one time offer (OTO) but may or may not schedule a booked call to speak with a sales team member about bigger opportunities made available to them throughout their funnel journey. A buyer lead is considered a premium lead regardless of whether or not they booked a call, because they already had enough confidence in the company or influencer to raise their hand and take their credit card out of their pocket and make a purchase. These leads are much more likely to be amenable to further upsells.

### Outbound Leads

Leads that go through a funnel and choose not to book a scheduled call at the time of their funnel journey are candidates for an outbound call. Closers typically do outbound calls to these leads when a scheduled appointment no shows or has to reschedule. These leads often bear fruit because they are educated about the opportunity. In many cases they are honored that someone from the team reached out to them. It gives them a chance to ask any question they may have had and get their concerns resolved so they can make a buying decision. It is also a great way to keep the sales team in the rhythm of selling when they have down time between scheduled calls.

## Learning Resources

Although it is not necessary to be an expert in the offer you are selling, it is extremely helpful to be very familiar with it. Having a basic knowledge of the offer gives the closer confidence when they get on the sales call.

A great way to boost this confidence is to make the offer content available to the sales team. This could be in the form of an online course, a private Facebook group, a private forum, access to live streams, group training calls or live webinars.

## Offer Stack

When shopping for a computer, phone or the latest gadget it is helpful to have a snapshot of the options available; a visual menu of your products or services. This includes how they compare with one another and at what price point, so you can see what fits your budget and what features and benefits meet your needs or wants.

The same type of visual snapshot is extremely helpful for closers when positioning an offer to fit their prospects goals and financial ability. It is recommended to have a simple chart to see all the options at a glance. This offer stack is a way to increase both the perceived and actual value of the offer you are making:

Chapter 4: Clarity on the Funnel and Offer

## Offer Descriptions

To fully clarify what is included with each item of the offer stack it is helpful to have a brief summary of what each line item entails. For example:

**30 Day Elite Success Course** - The 30 Day course consists of 30 chapters of content. Each chapter has 3 modules that take an average of 30 minutes to complete. Students should plan to spend about 90 minutes per day in the course to progress at the most rapid rate. To ensure the content is consumed, understood and can be implemented, only one chapter will be released each day. It will only be released if all content is complete. To measure understanding and completion, a short quiz will be given at the end of each module.

**Support** - 24/7 chat support via course portal. 1-800-000-0000 support line Monday thru Friday 9:00 a.m. to 6:00 p.m. Mountain time. Saturday 10:00 a.m. to 3:00 p.m. Mountain time. Closed Sunday.

**Group Coaching** - Held the first Thursday of every month from 7:00 p.m. to 8:30 p.m. Mountain time on Zoom. A link will be posted

### Randall Grizzle & Deborah Burris

in the community forum an hour prior to the meeting.

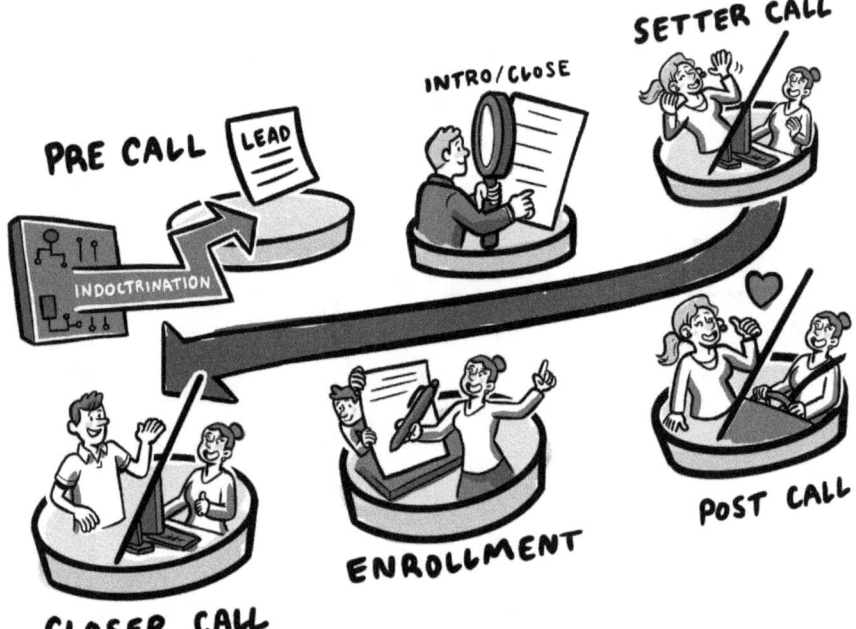

# Chapter 5: Intentional Sales Process

*"If you can't describe what you are doing as a process, you don't know what you are doing."*

-W. Edward Deming

To maximize the effectiveness of any high ticket sales strategy, you should have a crystal clear intentional sales process, including all touch points and goals. This is best mapped out in visual format so it's easy to understand exactly how your leads will reach each goal within your process.

At each stage of your intentional sales process you should consider the following elements:

- Thoughts, feelings, and needs of your prospect
- Actions your prospect will take
- Pain points that need to be alleviated
- Actions you and your team must take to help your prospect move through the flow

## Pre-Call

Whether the call is outbound or inbound, the prospect needs to receive communication so they are clear on when and where the call is happening. With most scheduling software, automated emails can be sent with all of these details. Some scheduling software has the capability to send SMS reminders as well. Unless these SMS reminders can be directly tied to the sales team member's work number, it is recommended they be turned off. If a prospect responds to these texts, the closer will not receive the response.

Automations can be set up with each closer's work phone number using the calling system to send pre-call text reminders that will allow the closer to receive and respond to the prospect's communication, keeping everything in alignment. It is recommended to send out a SMS confirmation from the closer's number at the time of booking, as well as one hour prior to the scheduled call time.

This pre-call communication can be a good way to interact with the prospect, even before speaking with them. The pre call SMS message can reflect the tone of the influencer or offer. Whether it be professional and serious, or fun and engaging, keeping a consistent tone helps posture the closer all the way through the close. If the customer responds to the SMS, responding back can help solidify them showing up to the call.

## Sales Methodologies

There are two main sales methodologies: Intro/Close and Set/Close. They both have their advantages and can be employed to best suit the offer and sales team members.

### Intro/Close

The Intro Close model is where one team member interacts with the customer from the beginning to the end of the sales process. In this model the sales professional can close the prospect on the first call or they can use the first call to set the stage for the deal, give the prospect some homework and schedule a second call to close the deal.

This model works well for lower ticket offers where the probability of a prospect showing up for a second call is low, and/or the opportunity cost of spending time on two scheduled calls with a prospect is too high.

# Chapter 5: Intentional Sales Process

## Set/Close

The two part sales process or Set/Close model is a time tested model. In this model, the setter prequalifies and "sets the stage" for the closer to be in the best position possible to close the deal. This prequalification focuses primarily on ensuring the prospect understands the offer and is financially qualified to move forward. In many cases it is helpful for the setter to provide homework for the client to complete between the set and the close.

Effective client homework helps the client get to the heart of WHY they are seeking change. It also sharpens their focus on the opportunity cost of not taking action. Some recommended homework questions include:

- What are your 3 month goals?
- What are your 6 month goals?
- What are your 12 month goals?
- What happens if you don't achieve these goals?
- How will achieving these goals impact your life and the lives of those you care about?
- Why does this change matter to you?

Think of the closer as being up to bat, the setter is standing firm on the pitching mound. Both the batter and pitcher are anxious to perform at the highest level. The pitcher winds up and throws the perfect pitch. The batter connects and hits a home run! That perfect pitch allowed the batter to hit it out of the park. Similarly, most high ticket closers know that the deal is actually done in the set.

The closer's main role is to ensure the prospect is willing to make the commitment necessary to have a reasonable expectation of success with the offer, to collect payment, and to provide a seamless transition to the customer success team.

## Post Call

After the sale is made it is very important to nurture the customer. This includes making sure they have a clear understanding of how to access the course material, support, and connect with the community. The customer success team typically handles this by making a welcome call. It is also highly recommended that the closer reaches out to the customer within 24 hours of the sale. This call is primarily to celebrate with them, make them feel like a part of the team, encourage them, and express confidence in their ability to succeed. While some closers like to keep business relationships with the new clients, this is where it needs to be made clear that it will be the customer success team, or fulfillment team that is their new point of contact. This post-closer call is sometimes referred to as the "jacuzzi" call, because all the big decisions have been made, the onboarding is complete, and it's now time to relax and celebrate before the hard work begins.

## Payment Processing Protocols

There are multiple ways to take payments for orders. Some offers allow maximum flexibility by having a shared link for the team to access payment processors (like Stripe) where sales team members can charge payments. This can be done as a full payment on one card or broken up into smaller payments on multiple cards to best fit the customer's needs. Payment links can also be used and configured to trigger fulfillment.

Wire transfers can also be used and are recommended for larger amounts. From the time the wire is sent by the customer, it typically takes 3 to 5 business days for the funds to reach the business account.

The most important thing with payments is that the process is clearly defined for the closer, and the expectation for what happens after the payment has cleared is clearly established and understood by the customer. This will keep the positive momentum going from the sales department to the customer success department. It will also make future payment collections much easier. Sales people by nature are people pleasers, so putting on the bail bondsman collection hat is usually not a fun day, and can easily be avoided with clear expectations from the beginning.

## Enrollment

Successful enrollment can take many forms. For simple offers it is often enough to have an email trigger a link and instructions to access the course content. For more complicated offers, it is recommended to have a dedicated team to hop on a call and walk the customer through logging into the course, joining the community, and navigating through all of the support avenues available to them.

Individuals on the enrollment team should be confident, friendly and patient. Things that will be intuitive to some customers will take a little extra effort for others to grasp.

It is highly recommended that the enrollment team focus on servicing the customer at the highest level and avoid upselling them on any other products or services.

## Customer Success

The more a customer feels supported the more favorably they will view your offer and company regardless of the rate at which they achieve their own personal success. We have seen countless customers across multiple market sectors become raving fans of companies because they felt supported, cared about, and nurtured after the sale.

A supported customer knows whether or not they are doing their part to win. They will correct themselves and regroup in private if they feel they are falling short. On the contrary, if they feel like they have been dropped like a hot potato as soon as their credit card has been processed, they will be very public in their disapproval.

> *When Randall and I meet with prospects there are two main things we are looking for during our initial discovery call: 1. Does the company offer something truly useful? 2. What do they have in place after the sale to help their customers succeed? It is amazing to work with companies that are so dedicated to fulfillment and so in tune with their customers. I recall one extraordinary incident where a husband died but wanted his wife to complete the journey they had started together. The wife was devastated by her loss but was determined to move forward. The company became aware of her situation and extended not only their condolences but a massive amount of support to help her succeed. Having solid fulfillment is the #1 thing a company can do ensure its longevity.*
>
> *DB*

# Chapter 6: Element of a Winning Script

*"Success is the sum of small efforts, repeated day in and day out."*

-Robert Collier

A winning script guides qualified prospects to a buying decision and preserves the energy of the sales team. Even when an influencer brings in a top tear closer, it is important to be able to provide them with a script. It's not because the closer doesn't know how to sell. It is because the team as a whole needs structure.

Before we get into the nitty-gritty of how the sales script process works, it's important to understand a few things. The number one sales tip we can give is time management. A high level sales closer will value their time and understand how to use it properly. They need to decipher the few curious from the serious. This is done by separating the different types of "apples".

If people were like apples, we would sort them into three general buckets. The first bucket we call the "sour" or "bad" apples. This doesn't mean bad people, but they are living in a situation with uncontrollable conditions. We know from experience that 30-40% of the prospects are sour apples. They are currently living with extenuating circumstances that would hold them back from getting started (ie: lack of resources, inability to make the time commitment, or simply are not a good fit for the offer). It is important to identify these people as soon as possible to eliminate the time constraint that comes with working on something that is flat out not going to happen.

The next bucket is the red apples. Everyone loves red apples. These are what the industry calls the "lay downs". They are the people that show up on the call pre-sold, and (provided the closer doesn't say something stupid) are going to buy. Red apples are easy to identify right from the beginning. A couple of good questions, and the red apples separate themselves. Typically 10-20% of leads are these delicious red apples.

That now leaves 50-70% of the remaining people who showed interest in your product to be put in this last bucket. These are the green apples. They are the people who can go either way. This is where the sales professionals earn their money. These green apples are the reason it is vital to have a script outline and focused dialogue. It's these leads that fall in this bucket that really separate the good closers from the great ones. There are buyers in this bucket. It is up to the sales person to walk them through the process and show them that this product can help them.

At different times, and with different offers, we have all found ourselves sorted into any of these three buckets.

## Chapter 6: Element of a Winning Script

> *I'm sure we have all been hit up by the "do this for a friend and they will receive $" lead tactic. My sister-in-law thoughtfully put down my wife and my name for a timeshare opportunity. As it was, we didn't have anything going on that Saturday morning and knew that it would help my sister-in-law out to spend the hour of our time for the $100 that she would receive. On our way to the event my newlywed wife and I were in the car talking about how we are doing this for her sister and we are NOT buying anything. We were on the same page and the deal was sealed with a fist bump. We walked in there confidently as sour apples.*
>
> *We sat through the 30 minute video that did a pretty good job showing the beauty of their resorts and accommodations. I could see it in both of us, that apple was turning a little more green than sour. Then we were ushered into the lion's den, the saleroom. We were met by an older, sweet, well polished lady who talked about how the #1 cause of divorce, is couples not spending enough time together. She built value, comparing what a once a year a-la carte vacation would cost, vs the annual expense of a timeshare. How the opportunity would be there for us to spend the time together and avoid that ugly "D" word.*
>
> *Well, two hours after we had our confident fist bump of no deal, my wife and I walked out of the venue as happy new timeshare vacation ownership members. Not only were we "just" members, we bought the upgraded option with the higher tier of locations. The good news is, we are still married and we still use the time share.*     *RG*

## Winning Script Framework

The sales script is simply an outline for a real conversation to determine if working together is going to create a win win relationship. From the example above, the sale would not have happened if the salesperson would have sat us down and read off a list of questions.

A script provides a framework so the conversation can flow naturally to uncover why the person booked the call, where they are at now, where they want to go and how we can help get them there. The elements of a winning script are: Introduction, Probe, Blast Pre Qualification Commitments, the Close and Onboarding.

## Introduction

This is the first human contact with the customer. The closer needs to make an impression. They need to create an attractive character presence and focus on building rapport with the prospect. This is the crucial part of the call where the closer sets the pace, using voice fluctuation, tempo and energy for the call. They need to be present and demonstrate to the prospect that they are a credible authority to help find a solution for their problems.

## Probe

This is the most important part of the call process. Asking for a "Readers Digest" version of where they are at is a great way to start the interview into their struggles. It's asking them to talk about themselves and to express their pain and their struggle. Let the customer do the talking while guiding the conversation with thoughtful questions. Where are they in their journey? What do they need help with? What have been their roadblocks? And most importantly, what needs to happen for them to get the results they desire? Avoid the "yes" or "no" questions and ask them in a way that gets them talking.

## Blast

This third part of the script outline is where the salesperson shows the value of what your company can provide. The blast is your story and creates the excitement for change. What is it that your product/service can do better than anyone else? How is your product going to ease the struggle of your customer?

# Chapter 6: Element of a Winning Script

## Commitments

Every solution to any problem they have is going to require commitments on both ends. Your business is going to work to help solve their problems, but this is a partnership and they need to be willing to do their part to help themselves as well. It is important for them to know that in order to be successful, they will need to commit to a few things on their end. With the decision to make changes, comes these four commitments:

**Time.** Nothing is an overnight fix. Are they willing to put in the work? Are they willing to take the time required to gain the knowledge and finish what they start?

**Knowledge.** Are they open minded and teachable? Are they willing to admit that they don't know what they don't know, and be comfortable in a student-teacher relationship?

**Decision Making**: Here is where the sales team needs to make sure the decision makers are involved on the call. Is there anyone else that needs to be in on this process? Spouse? Business partner? The goal is to put them in the best position possible, without excuses, to make a decision with the closer on that call. When the proper decision makers are not there, you end up playing a bad game of telephone, and your chances of closing the deal without a same day decision goes down exponentially.

**Financial Investment**: The prospect needs to understand that this will be an exchange of value. Your business is providing valuable resources to get them from where they are to where they want to be. In exchange, there will be a financial investment. Can the prospect afford that financial investment needed for your services? Is the money accessible and ready to invest, or will they need time to gather funds from an outside source?

This script outline will help sales team members guide the prospect to a decision to buy. While this guide is step-by-step better than reading from pages of a script, it is the closer who will need to make sure the prospect really knows and understands their pain. This means becoming a good interviewer and letting the prospect talk. They need to build a relationship and let the person share where they are vulnerable. Let them feel the pain of their own situation.

> *My family is centered around being active. We like our activities and engaging in sports. I had a "Fit by Forty" goal, I wanted to be a specific weight by my 40th birthday and I got within a pound or three of hitting it. The birthday came and went. I was proud of my success, even if I didn't hit the exact number, it still meant I lost 42 pounds. Time went on and as it did I lost my focus on my weight. One day I decided to step on a scale and I was wrecked by the number and I knew it was time to make changes again. I went to the crossfit gym my wife goes to consistently. I used to be a member but that was two years and xx pounds ago. When I sat down with the owner we talked about getting my health back. We didn't talk about exercises he could have me do, or meal plans I could follow. No. We talked about my family. We talked about my concerns of being where I was at with my longevity. He tapped into my emotions and got me teared up. I not only committed to coming back to the gym on the spot, I also committed to 1-on-1 training with him as my coach.* — RG

People will buy when they have an attachment to the value they are being presented with. If we want to get people to make decisions they wouldn't normally make, it is critical that we get them into an emotional state. The structure is there for a guideline, but the presentation needs to mean something to the client.

## Close

All the previous work is about to come together when the client is led through the labyrinth and they are ready to Close. This is where all the loose strings are tied into a bow and a new client will be welcomed into the program. Don't get me wrong, not every call will get to this point, but when it does, this is where following the above process properly will pay off. The situation is thoroughly under control, there is an in-depth understanding of the prospects' pain and goals and they are asking for the next steps to get started.

## Chapter 6: Element of a Winning Script

The process of ASK and LISTEN and ASK again are crucial. There needs to be a poise and authority during this phase as the closer will be asking for delicate information from the client, namely their credit card number. A lot of people hold this info tight to their chest. It is very important for them to feel as comfortable as possible when you're collecting personal information. This is a sensitive process where the closer must "hold hands" with the client to keep the assurance that their time, money, and decision to make the investment, was in fact the right one.

## Onboarding

Once the transaction has been approved, there needs to be a clear path and a smooth transition to getting started with the program. People will ultimately buy your product because they believe the purchase makes sense. The Closer has done their job to get the client excited, it is now your job to make sure the fulfillment is in place.

This is the relay, the "hand-off of the baton" if you will. It is crucial that things are smooth and seamless. This starts a new beginning for the client and the hand holding needs to continue until they are comfortable with their decisions and gain confidence in your business. The Closer needs to have clear direction on the next steps to communicate to the client. When will they be getting a call from your company? Who will the client be talking to? What are the exact next steps from there?

It will be natural for the client to have some doubts and second thoughts about their purchase. Having multiple touchpoints from the fulfillment team will help reassure the client regarding their purchase and ultimately reduce any anxiety they may be feeling.

# Chapter 7: Effective Call Execution

*"Some people want it to happen, some wish it would happen, others make it happen."*

-Michael Jordan

## Situational Role Play

While some of us have a natural talent for selling, no-one is born being a polished expert. So before you release your team "into the wild" to represent your company and generate sales, it's important to have them practice. This allows you to see how they perform in situations they're likely to encounter with prospects, ensure they are representing your brand as intended, and correct any potential deficiencies. These role play experiences also help your sales team build confidence in their abilities. Here are some tips to maximize the effectiveness of this exercise for your team.

### Use a structured format

Don't make the mistake of "winging it". You need to ensure you and your team are exposed to the most likely scenarios that can occur with prospects. Include all stages of your sales process in your role play scenarios, including first contact, making the sale, and post-sale follow-up.

Include different customer personalities in your role play scenarios

Your closers will encounter a wide variety of people during their sales calls, and they need to be able to handle them all with ease:

- The "yeah but…" customer (they have objections, sometimes a lot of them — ensure your team is comfortable overcoming these)
- The "detail-oriented" customer (they want to know every last detail about your product or service. It's critical for your sales team to be intimately familiar with what they're selling, down to the tiniest details)
- The "savvy" customer (they are very familiar with what you and your competitors offer. Your team must be able to close the deal, showing why your offering is the best)
- The "commitment-phobe" (the customer seems to love your offer, but won't commit. Teach your team how to reassure these prospects so they are comfortable enough to buy)
- The "distrusting customer" (they may be worried about getting duped, or be suspicious that your team is trying to upsell them something they don't truly need. Your team should avoid becoming offended, know when to ask for the sale versus when to back off, and be skilled at addressing all customer concerns with integrity and professionalism)

### Include all types of objections in your role play exercises

Internal objections — These are concerns the customer has about their own ability to benefit from the product. For example, they may be worried they aren't skilled or knowledgeable enough to use the product.

External objections — These are concerns the customer has about outside forces that are beyond their control. For example, they may worry they don't have the time to make use of your product or service, they may worry about the market or economy changing in a way that would negate the benefits of your product, etc.

Product or service concerns — This category of objections relates to worries your prospects may have about your offering. For example, they may wonder if your product or service is actually as good as you say it is, and if it will really solve their problem and deliver results.

### Effective role play prepares your sales team for success

Ensure your team is comfortable and highly skilled in every aspect of your sales process. The result of this thorough training is that you can trust them to represent your brand in a positive way, and be confident they'll make the most of every sales situation.

## Embrace Your Native Genius

Each closer is unique. Authenticity and sincerity are keys to building trust with your audience, and are especially important when you ask them to part with their money and buy.

Prospects will notice if salespeople seem like they're acting a part, or being someone they're not. For that reason, the best thing you can do is allow your team the freedom to be themselves, and to let their unique personalities shine through (even though they will still need to adhere to the general guidelines for how to handle themselves).

Here are some of the ways your closers can embrace their own native genius to maximize their success as they represent your brand during the sales process. And if you're doing sales calls yourself, all of this advice applies to you as well.

### Don't copy someone else's style

All too often, salespeople fall into the trap of copying someone else's style to the point that they come across as too scripted and inauthentic. For example, when someone who is naturally reserved tries to be gregarious and loud, odds are that this "performance" will be perceived as fake. Worse, when we pretend to be someone we're not, we tend to lack confidence. This makes the entire interaction awkward for all parties involved.

Counsel your salespeople to be themselves. Whether your closer has a light-hearted personality, is somewhat reserved, or is a classic outgoing extrovert, all can be successful in sales provided they make the most of their strengths in interpersonal interactions.

## Use scripts only as a guide

When someone is reading verbatim from a script, we pick up on it right away. It sounds a bit too perfect and at its worst, it comes across as monotonous and robotic. The solution is for your sales team to internalize the script to the point where they make it their own. This means they'll cover all the key points in the script, but in a way that sounds natural and authentic.

> *Being a rookie on the sales floor I wanted to do all the right things. At the time, it was my first sales job, and I was instructed to dial the numbers and read from "this" script. I was getting a few deals, but by no means killing it with my numbers. It was about a month into the job when a vetran team leader walked up to me, took the sales script from my hands, threw it on the ground and said "you don't need this." He then proceeded to tell me that the script is meant to be a guide, not a word for word recording. The sales would come from the connection that is created by the closer. And reading directly from a piece of paper is not going to connect with anyone.*
>
> *RG*

Using situational role play as discussed earlier is a great way for your team to learn how to use any scripts you've prepared as an outline for genuine, sincere conversations with prospects and customers.

## Remember that relationships drive sales

People buy from those they know, like, and trust. And the key to becoming that person in the eyes of prospects is for closers to be themselves in all interactions. After all, people don't tend to warm up to cookie-cutter, robotic, fake salespeople trying to fit into someone else's idea of who they should be. In contrast, they buy from interesting people who are genuine enough to earn their trust. They

## Chapter 7: Effective Call Execution

buy from people they enjoy interacting with. They buy from people who make them feel comfortable and at ease. The best way to accomplish this is to embrace the fact that every closer is unique and will perform best by leaning into their own native genius in all sales interactions.

## Review Recordings

One of the best ways to improve the results of sales calls fast is to listen to your own call recordings and/or watch your video sales calls. The reason for this is that actually hearing yourself speak will have a far more memorable lasting impact on improving your handling of future calls, compared to having someone else merely give you a list of tips for improvement. However, tips for improvement still have a role to play because knowing what to look out for is key.

With that in mind, here are some things to consider as you listen to your own sales calls. This of course, applies to every member of your sales team, since they should also be listening to their own calls. Before you begin, keep in mind that you may have to listen to the call more than once to get the most out of this process.

### Start with the big picture

Listen to the overall tone of your voice to see if you sound approachable, friendly, and confident in your knowledge (but not arrogant). If you feel anything was off, work on improving it for your next call. Most people find that the simple act of being aware of any shortcomings puts them on the fast track for rapid improvement.

Next, take note of whether the call ended in the result you wanted (did you make the sale?).

### Analyze the customer's responses

Assess how they received the information you provided on the call.

- Did they understand what you meant?
- Did they seem to get more open towards your message as the call progressed, or did they withdraw?

- Did they sound impatient to end the call, or did they maintain interest from start to finish?

### Figure out how you might have improved your handling of the call

If the prospect ever seemed confused, consider how you could have worded things differently to avoid that.

If there were times when the call seemed to lose momentum or get awkward, think of ways you could have kept things moving.

If you had bad luck and the client seemed irritated or annoyed, was there anything you could have done differently to avoid this outcome?

If the customer didn't buy, can you pinpoint any portions of the conversation that could have changed that outcome if only you'd said something different?

### Take note of the things you did right

Looking for ways to improve is certainly important, but you also need to take notice of all the things you did well. This ensures you will continue to do those things, and make them an automatic habit going forward.

### Practice makes perfect

Role play (as discussed earlier) is helpful for practice, however, you can also do it on your own. Think of it as rehearsing a speech or presentation in front of the mirror, except in this case you're rehearsing snippets of conversation that might come up in future.

Practice the things you did right during the call until they feel easy and natural. And for those things you want to do differently, practice saying what you wish you'd said during the sales call until it too, becomes natural.

Finally, consider recording your practice so you can hear how you sound. Repeat the process until you're satisfied with the result.

## Chapter 7: Effective Call Execution

# Prepare for Common Objections

As you know, there are three common types of objections and you and your sales team need to be prepared for all of them: internal, external, and product/service concerns. Here is how to do it.

### Make a list

Start with a list of the most common objections or obstacles you're likely to encounter on a call. Some examples of what you might come up against are as follows:

- "It's too expensive."
- "I don't have time to use it."
- "I'm already using a product/service that does that, so I don't need yours."
- "Just send me some info."

When you make your own list, you should also include objections specific to your actual product or service. But in the meantime, here are some factors you should consider when you hear the more general objections.

### "It's too expensive."

There are several ways you can approach this, depending on the reasons behind their price objection:

- Focus on the reasons they reached out to investigate the offer in the first place.
- Reflect on their Why!
- Anchor back to their goals and their pain.
- Discuss the opportunity cost of inaction.
- Explore financial options they have available to them.
- If your product or service can "pay for itself", explain how. This is a great time to pull out case studies demonstrating how other clients saved money or made more money thanks to your solution.

- Find out if you can follow up with them at a later date when cash flow is better for them.

You should also consider the fact that price is not always the real reason they are objecting. Sometimes the underlying issue is they simply don't fully understand the value you are providing. This can be solved by providing the information they require to realize your offer is a great fit for them.

### "I don't know if I have time."

Oftentimes, not having enough free time is a driving factor in why someone is looking to make a change in their life. If you have done a good enough job digging into their pain points, they will be willing to sacrifice their time now, for a better life down the road. Remind them that if they want to see the change, they have to BE the change. After all, the definition of insanity is "doing the same thing over and over again, expecting a different result" (Albert Einstein). Also make sure that they understand the time commitment required, and if it can be structured around their own schedule. A lot of the time this can be cleared up by setting the proper expectations right up front.

### "Let me think about it"

Let me think about it is probably the most common objection of all. Respectfully ask how long they have been thinking about making a change in their situation. Remind them there is a reason they identified with this offer and took the time to schedule a call with you. It is usually because they have known for years they need to do something different to get out of debt and save for the goals they have for themselves and the ones they care about. The reality is that they are on the call with a closer because they have already decided they need to make a change. They are looking at your offer as the vehicle to make that change. Your confidence in what you are selling is the #1 factor in them making a buying decision. Be strong. Be confident. Be the voice that gives them the courage to commit to the change they knew they needed to make when booking the call with you.

## Chapter 7: Effective Call Execution

"Just send me some information."

This response sometimes serves as a classic brush off, when people don't feel comfortable saying they aren't interested. Other times, it's used when people simply don't know what they're missing. If the offer has a strong pre-call indoctrination and sales process this will never be a viable objection.

### Preparing for objections in advance helps you handle them with success

The last thing you want, is to find yourself or your sales team stuttering with uncertainty or a loss for words when your prospect throws an objection your way. Instead, transform objections into opportunities to better educate them and improve your overall presentation. The best way to do this is to figure out what your customers will worry about before they say it, so you're 100% prepared to address their concerns with a polished response that moves them closer to a buying decision.

## Effective Visual Pitch Techniques

When a voice call is all you need to close the sale, that's great. But sometimes you need to go a step further to convince your prospect to buy. This is where visual pitch techniques come into play. Often it's helpful to *show* things about your product or service, rather than merely *talk* about it. Here are some of the ways you can incorporate visuals into your supplemental sales materials:

### Case studies

If you have permission to do so, share a flattering photo of a happy customer. This increases the credibility of the case study since there is a real person depicted. As part of your case study, show how things were before and after using your product or service (ideally there should be an obvious contrast between the two images, with the "after" image clearly being the ideal outcome).

## Workflow

If your service has a complex workflow, a visual flow chart is by far the easiest way to make it easy to understand. Similarly, if your product must be used in a certain way (and this can be broken down into a series of steps) a flow chart or product tour to demonstrate makes a great addition to your marketing materials.

## Features and benefits charts

Feature and benefit charts are a great way to show prospects all the ways your solution will help them. Charts are easy to skim over and include all necessary information in a visually appealing manner.

## Comparison charts

You can use these in several ways:

First, if you have multiple tiers of service or several product variations, you can use a comparison chart to help your prospects see which one is best for their needs.

Another great way to use comparison charts is to compare your offering to that of the competition. The goal here is to choose points of comparison that are flattering for your own product or service, and position your offering in the best possible light.

Finally, a twist on competition comparison charts is to use these charts to weed out customers who are not a good fit for your offering (because they can see at a glance whether your offering can do what they require). The flip side of this is that such charts also make it obvious to your ideal customers that yes, your product would be a fantastic fit for them.

## Repurposing

As you prepare your visual pitch deck, you should also keep an eye out for visuals that can be repurposed as social media images, handouts during live presentations, or included with product instruction manuals and the like. This allows you to get the most "bang for your buck" in exchange for the time and effort you put into creating these visuals.

## Graphics

For all the above cases, add relevant images to make them more attractive to look at, easier to understand (sometimes a picture is worth a thousand words), and serve as proof that your product or service does indeed do what you say it will. All photography should be of the highest quality, to show your product or service in the best possible way.

# Compliance

For any offer to provide a long term opportunity for the sales department, the company has to stay in business. In the world of High Ticket Sales, the fastest way to lose that opportunity is to be out of alignment in the area of compliance. Companies need to train their sales force to avoid making absolute claims. Teams need to provide reasonable evidence with statements that are truthful and not misleading to the prospect.

Several high profile companies in the High Ticket space have gone out of business for being out of integrity and making earnings claims. Earnings claims can be expressed or implied. An express earnings claim is where a closer tells the customer how quickly they are going to recoup their investment in the program and how much money they can expect to make in a specified period of time.

"You will see a full return of your investment in 6 months."

"You will earn enough to own a new Porsche within a year."

"You'll be able to buy that new house you wanted in the next two years."

Claiming extraordinary results by making specific claims that are not achieved by a substantial number of consumers is deceptive. Implied earnings claims lead people to believe they are going to be assured to have the same success as someone else in the program, or that by working with a 6 figure mentor they will make 6 figures. Testimonials and comparison stories can be used, but should be in conjunction with a disclosure that this might not be the case for everyone.

"Although these results are extraordinary, some of our current customers have made $5,000 a month or more each month using our system and we believe you can too."

Reasonably qualifying the individual you are selling is also a must. Predatory selling to the elderly or incompotent is not only wrong but will result in bad karma and a high probability the FTC will be knocking at your door.

# Chapter 8: Tools & Techniques for Optimal Performance

*"Be a yardstick of quality. Some people aren't used to an environment where excellence is expected."*

-Steve Jobs

The old saying "adapt or die" is true for sales teams. Gone are the days of boiler rooms full of closers, paper lead sheets, paper probe sheets, and compliance girls. Today's closers have to be willing to learn how to use technology in order to keep that line straight from the top to the bottom of the company to maximize profitability and serve customers at the highest level.

Likewise, savvy business owners will provide their sales teams with the best tools to streamline the sales process for their closers, ensure the best possible customer experience, and protect themselves from false claims.

These are the basic tools any business will have in place if they are serious about thriving, are proud of their organization, and are intent on providing long term service to their clients with a sustainable opportunity for their entire company:

- Company Branded Email
- Appointment Scheduling Platform
- Customer Relationship Management (CRM) System

- VoIP Phone System
- Team Communication Tools

## Company Branded Email

Have you ever asked a business what their email address is where they have responded with something like mycompany@gmail.com or napoleon.mycompany@gmail.com? These examples do not promote a feeling of competence or confidence in the company being around long term.

G Suite is a business-grade service offered by Google. It is a cloud-based platform perfect for growing companies. It is simple to set up, has business domain-based emails that are easy to manage, extremely affordable, and reliable. It also has additional security settings that can be managed at the admin level for the entire organization. This allows the company email to look much more professional, like firstname@mycompany.com.

When building a Playbook for your sales team you will most likely use Google Drive associated with your G Suite account to house sensitive documents. As closers join your team the only way they will be able to access these documents is through the company email you set up on their behalf. Likewise, if a closer is no longer with the company their email access will instantly be suspended or deleted making it impossible to access sensitive company information.

## Appointment Scheduling Platform

One of the most critical components of any High Ticket offer is a robust, reliable, and secure appointment scheduling platform. With more and more sales interactions happening virtually, it is critical the option you choose has a smooth seamless integration with the major video platforms out there, including Zoom, WebEx, Microsoft Teams, GoToMeeting, and Google Meet.

Choose an appointment scheduling option that can accommodate creating custom questions on your booking forms to capture more

## Chapter 8: Tools & Techniques for Optimal Performance

information about your prospect for the closer. If you have multiple lead types, you will most likely need multiple booking forms.

Each closer on your team will need their own booking page so they can set their availability; you can attach your companies booking rules and priorities to each closer's page. Each closer's booking page and corresponding availability is linked to their company domain email associated with your G Suite account.

Of the multiple scheduling options available we have found Once Hub to be the most stable platform with the greatest flexibility to manage the lead flow and closer priorities. It's reporting and integrations allow us to pull valuable data that we report to our clients so they can make decisions based on facts not feelings.

Another key feature we use consistently within Once Hub is its resource pool capabilities in Schedule Once. Putting closers in different resource pools based on lead type, gives us one more layer of control over where each lead goes, and provides the ability to make adjustments quickly. Putting leads in the right hands is key to maximizing profitability for the business.

## Customer Relationship Management (CRM)

One of the most important tools you can have to create clarity with your leads and sales team is use a Customer Relationship Management system, commonly referred to as a CRM. Your CRM can be customized to mirror your sales process so you have one central place to see how close your prospects are to turning into customers.

In addition to establishing a sales pipeline that mirrors your sales process, there are several other things a CRM can facilitate to ensure messaging is consistent, and all customer communication is visible within the leads contact record. Some of these features include shared team email templates, email signatures, activity logs to follow up on future customer actions, a place to record notes, dispositions for lost leads and drop down list for products.

If you are a business owner just launching your offer, a CRM will allow you to have a complete secure record of every lead you generate. Unlike a Google sheet, a CRM can add another layer of data security. Administrators of the CRM can prohibit downloading customer contact information ensuring your company data is not shared inappropriately. If you are a business owner who started out using spreadsheets and would like to gain more control over your data, transitioning to a CRM will give you much more peace of mind.

A good CRM will make it much easier for a sales person to work their leads through activity based selling practices, ensuring the investment you made in generating that lead is maximized. In short, if you are not using a CRM to manage your sales team, it is going to be extremely difficult to know how much revenue you are losing and be harder to identify where along the sales process improvements should be made to maximize conversions.

## Phone System

A reliable phone system is absolutely critical in today's sales environment. There are many Voice Over IP (VOIP) systems that seamlessly integrate with your CRM, offering you maximum flexibility to select the CRM and phone system that best suits your needs. Combining the functionality of your CRM and phone system will significantly streamline a closer's work day. This includes functions such as follow-up emails, moving deals, follow up sms, voicemail drops, etc. It can almost double the efficacy of your sales team.

Additionally, a phone system gives you full visibility into which team members are hitting the metrics for dials, talk time and total connections. Many systems have whisper mode, which allows you to not only monitor live calls, but actually communicate with the salesperson in real time during the call. This can be especially helpful when training new team members.

Recorded calls offer many benefits and can be accessed through your phone system portal and/or CRM for easy access. It can be helpful for setters and closers to review their recorded calls to learn where they could improve or overcome an objection in the future. It could also prove beneficial when using a setter/closer model. The closer can also listen to the set before jumping into their close, so that everyone is on the same page. Recording the calls may also be essential for compliance. It is important to remember to notify the prospect within the first minute or so of the conversation, that the call is being recorded.

Some business owners allow their sales teams to use their own personal cell phone numbers to cut costs. Doing this is like playing Russian roulette with your brand. This can lead to compliance and FTC issues. Most states require the following on each call: 1. State who you are 2. State the purpose of the call 3. State that the call is being recorded. If the FTC were to call your sales team posing as a customer to ensure you are in compliance, would they pass the test?

To control cost with your phone system, we recommend selecting an option that allows you unlimited calling for the most common geographic locations. This way you do not need to worry about "per minute" charges so you can encourage your sales team to follow up aggressively with every lead. Most phone systems that are natively built into CRM's do not offer unlimited calling for one fixed rate, nor does it offer the robust capabilities of a phone system that can easily be integrated. We recommend using the "a la carte" approach to ensure you get maximum efficiencies and cost savings by choosing and connecting the best in class of each tool.

## Team Communication

In today's fast pace global remote sales environment it is critical to be able to organize your team communication. Here are some tools that can simplify your process and create efficiencies for your sales team.

### Slack

For internal company communication Slack is our #1 recommendation. Slack allows you to segment communication into various channels. For example: you can have private channels for management communication, and public channels for sales team communication, leaderboards, fulfillment and customer support. Through Slack you can make phone calls and video chat with team members around the world.

Slack has native integrations for commonly used programs like Google Docs and Google Sheets. It also has an API that allows you to connect many tools like Hello Sign via Zapier.

### Voxer

Voxer is the perfect tool for quick communication. It is the modern day version of a walkie talkie. In this busy age we need to keep our communication short and precise. Voxer is the perfect tool to help do that. Sometimes a phone call is not needed and you just want to send a quick voice message to someone. Voxer allows you to get right to the point and have your audio message delivered immediately.

We recommend this communication tool be used for more time-sensitive or urgent communication.

### Zoom

Zoom has taken the video conferencing world by storm. Video conferencing is the perfect medium for sales team meetings, customer engagements, and one on ones. There is a reason why Zoom is now the number one video conferencing platform on the planet. It is reliable and is recommended as the "go to" communication tool for web conferencing. You can start with a free account and upgrade as your team grows.

## Integration: Zapier

Without going into geek territory, most of the systems we recommend have an open Application Programming Interface (API) that allows other systems to talk to each other. Sometimes it can be a difficult task to create a direct integration with all of these systems. Zapier changed the game by providing a platform to easily build integration between multiple systems. A real popular saying by one of the leading CRM companies back in 2013 was "we are an all-in-one solution". That was good at the time until Zapier came along. Zapier allows you to create the "BEST IN BREED" solution without being pigeon-holed into an all-in-one solution. Now you can easily purchase the best CRM, Email Autoresponder, Shopping Cart Solution, Calling/texting feature and integrate these solutions into one system using Zapier. Zapier has changed the game forever. Zapier is not the only system out there. Other solutions include Microsoft Flow,

Workato, Automate, Inegromat. Do your research and find the best integration software that meets your needs.

The purpose of having any, or all, of these systems and tools is organization. Keeping track of the details is not as difficult when it's a small handful of people working around you, as you work to grow your business. However, as business gets bigger the client list scales with the business. When you have larger teams working remotely, there needs to be tools and systems in place to manage the flow of information. Having these tools in place will help you run your business more efficiently, so you can spend your time ON the business and not IN the business.

## User and Security Protocols

It is recommended to keep a master sheet of sales team member's contact information and tool access that is accessible to the administrator only. It is helpful to have this information to track access of regular users and team leaders. When onboarding and offboarding users, it is helpful to have a central place to ensure each user is connected or disconnected from each tool.

It is recommended that each user changes their password quarterly in each tool for security purposes. Providing detailed, written instructions on how to do this along with loom video tutorials is very helpful. These instructions can be kept in F.O.C.U.S. Resources (more on this in chapter 10).

# Chapter 9: Effective Sales Meetings & Reviews

*"What gets measured, gets managed."*

-Peter Drucker

Sales meetings and performance reviews should be positive and energetic. Even when improvements are needed, approaching them from a solution oriented mindset will yield the best results.

## Know Your Numbers

The sales score is entirely by the numbers. It is absolutely critical that the sales team has confidence in the numbers being reported. Smart sales professionals will keep their own sales records so they can trust but verify those being reported by sales management. At the beginning of each week the first order of business is to report the sales numbers for the previous week. This gives the sales leadership an opportunity to give a shout out to performers, announce any spiffs/bonuses they may have won, and provides a set time for team members to congratulate and celebrate those that had a great week.

Taking the time to review the sales numbers as a team facilitates time for feedback. The team members can discuss how prospects are responding to any changes that may have been implemented in the funnel or sales process.

## Sales Leaderboard

In addition to having a formal team review of the numbers on a team meeting, it is also extremely effective to have a sales leaderboard that is updated (at least) daily. You'll find the top salespeople are also some of the most competitive people. Seeing the numbers will drive them. This leaderboard should be accessible at all times to the entire sales team. When performance is measured and openly visible to peers it incentivizes excellence.

### Effort Based Metrics

Although score is kept in dollars sold, there may be a lag collecting payments due to various reasons. However, there is always a correlation that those doing the work and putting in the dials and talk time are at the top of the leaderboard.

Posting the number of dials and total talk time on a weekly basis will underscore why those receiving the highest compensation are being handsomely rewarded. It will also put those that are not performing on notice that they need to step up their efforts to keep the opportunity.

Each team member should have at least 3 hours of talk time or 100 dials daily if they expect to receive a generous full-time income.

## Pipeline Management

Keeping tabs on who is managing their pipeline effectively is important to ensure that each lead is honored. A full lead pack of scheduled application appointments is considered to be 20 to 30 leads per week. If a team member has stewardship over this number of leads weekly and does not move each lead along the sales pipeline after each customer interaction, it will be impossible for them to "remember" what they need to do to serve that lead at the highest level.

Check each sales team members pipeline weekly to ensure they are moving leads through the process toward the close. Periodically run reports to show where each team member's leads are in the pipeline and make those reports visible to the sales team.

## Express Gratitude

Sales is a zero to hero business. The highs can be exhilarating but the lows can be rather lonely especially in a remote work environment. Sales management should actively look for wins each team member is having and recognize those wins. These wins don't necessarily have to be all about the numbers. It could be recognizing them for going above and beyond to help a customer or someone in another department. During team meetings invite team members to give shout-outs to each other as well. Positivity is contagious! A performing team will give compliments freely and accept compliments graciously.

Think outside the box and get creative! This can be SWAG gear for the new person to make them feel welcomed to the team. Sending cookies or edible treats to members who are having a tough day or family surgeries.

*I am truly blessed to have the most amazing assistant on the planet! She works tirelessly to help things run smoothly for our teams. I know I can always count on her to get things done and it frees my mind and time to work on things that create efficiencies for our clients to expand their businesses. I am truly grateful for her. She is so amazing she often minimizes her own needs. It came to my attention that she had some health struggles. That combined with the pressure of running a household amidst COVID limitations and juggling business responsibilities gave way to a particularly stressful day. The remedy that seemed appropriate was a special delivery of cookies and milk. We received a picture of the open box of cookies along with a message that the entire family was delighted by the gesture. It wasn't about the cookies and milk, although they were a big hit. It was all about feeling cared for and special that we took the time to show how grateful we are for her.*

*I make it a point to express gratitude on a regular basis to team members by giving them a shout out in a Slack team channel, sending them a private message, or giving them a call. Simply recognizing them or remembering a special event that is going on in their life or the lives of their family builds unity and loyalty.*

*I have also been the recipient of those who wished to express the gratitude for my contributions. On my birthday a magnificent arrangement of flowers was delivered to my home office. They were from one of our high performing sales teams. I was absolutely overcome with gratitude at their thoughtful act. Sometimes in life something simple happens that makes a lasting impact. For me this was one of those moments. It made me think of even more ways I could ensure rich opportunities for them in the future. You know who you are.* DB

Chapter 9: Effective Sales Meetings & Reviews

## Encourage Sharing

The scarcity sales mindset is to keep "all the good stuff" to yourself to maintain a competitive advantage. Encourage team members to share what is working for them and what they are struggling with so that everyone can benefit. This is best facilitated by open and honest communication throughout the organization. Establishing an environment of transparency builds trust and confidence. This feeling of security will help team members open up and share.

## Provide Leadership Opportunity

As the sales team grows, leaders within the team will rise up and want to take on a bigger role within the team structure. This is a sign of a healthy team. Encourage this by providing opportunities for these individuals to be team leaders.

This could take the form of having several micro teams within sales teams that support and rely on each other. Micro teams can get into a rhythm where there is a synergistic effect with sales because team members know exactly what is expected and how they can best maximize their role within that smaller team.

Some team members may take a special interest in mentoring new team members, holding specific skills training outside the regular meetings, or do a special training during a team sales meeting.

## Encourage Business Owner Interaction

Understanding the Business Owner's "Why" is powerful. It is highly encouraged to have the business owner come on the sales meeting at least once per month to stay connected with the pulse of the team. Sharing the story of why the company and offer exists will help the sales team feel like part of the company family. It will help improve sales because people like to know who they are doing business with.

Sales team members know the value of their time, so they especially understand the value of the company leaders. Business owners should take the opportunity to come on the meetings monthly to share customer successes, exciting new things the company is doing to add more value to the customer and to express sincere appreciation for the members of the sales team. This is the time for them to not only share their direction and ideas, but also welcome comments from the sales team. After all, they are the ones who are the first direct contact with the prospective buyers.

> *One of the experiences I remember the most from my time at a company is when the Vice President of the company took the time out of their day to talk to our sales team. I provided some feedback on what I was seeing from the customers and made suggestions for improvements from my perspective. The VP of the company told me that my job was "not to come up with ideas. Just sell." I never looked at the VP, or the company, the same again. That experience ruined my enthusiasm for the company.*     *RG*

It is important to not only spend the time with the sales team, but also to make them feel important. Engage with them in a conversation and not just instructions or directions. Obviously, not all ideas need to be used, but ideas should not be dismissed or diminished. The machine of a business runs most efficiently when all of the parts work together.

## Effective Closer Performance Reviews

Holding regular performance reviews individually with each team member provides an opportunity for two way feedback. We typically do reviews every 6 weeks. There can be variables in performance due to having a off week, a change in the funnel, etc. But we have found that a 6 week average of the numbers is an accurate measure of overall performance, and a good time frame to make any corrections to get that team member back on track.

The most important part of these reviews is active listening. Team members can provide great feedback on how to improve the overall

## Chapter 9: Effective Sales Meetings & Reviews

customer experience. They can give constructive input on how management can help them serve the customers at a higher level.

It is an opportunity to create a deeper connection with that team member and express sincere gratitude for the strengths they bring to the team.

"F.O.C.U.S."

# Chapter 10: F.O.C.U.S. Resources

*"Patience, persistence and perspiration make an unbeatable combination for success.*

-Napoleon Hill

## Frequently Occurring Customer and User Situations (F.O.C.U.S.)

Creating a dedicated, organized, resource area will empower the sales team to find the answers they need to close deals and support customers. Sometimes it is difficult to remember what to do in each situation in the middle of customer interaction. Having a specific place to know "What to do" when "xyz"" happens, brings a lot of peace of mind to the team.

## Closer Support

Closers may need support in the following areas:

- What do I do when I have a duplicate lead?
- What if one of my payment plans fails?
- Who do I contact if survey responses did not come through on the form?

- How do I know where the lead originated?
- How can I tell if a payment was processed successfully?
- Can I see if someone purchased a tripwire offer prior to my scheduled call?
- How do I reset the passwords for my tools and systems?

## Customer Support

- Who do I reach out to if I have a question about the product or program?
- How do I get a copy of my receipt?
- How long does my preferred support access last?
- How do I log into my training portal?

# Chapter 11: Winning Based on Fact Not Emotion

*"Successful people do what unsuccessful people are not willing to do. Don't wish it were easier; wish you were better. "*

-Jim Rohn

## Sustainable Success is in the Numbers

At this point we have gotten the customer's attention. We have gotten them to raise their hand, and asked for, at least, a conversation about the ability to grow and change their current situation. We have indoctrinated them, taught them about who we are and how we can help. We are in the process of leading them down a path for success. But what about your company? Are you keeping the details needed to help your numbers grow? The success of your company is not in the first contact with the customer, it's in the follow up. Your ability to make decisions based on facts and not emotions are key to creating long-term opportunity for your business and sales team.

In the process of working to grow and help High Ticket businesses, we have had multiple conversations with business owners about scaling up their current success. These owners will know about their gross profit. They will know about their ad spend. They might even know how many leads they get a week.

But what stumps them, every time, is the details of their numbers. Most business owners struggle to answer the following questions:

- "What is your current conversion rate?"
- "What regions do you have the most effective ad spend?"
- "What is the major reason your leads aren't converting?"
- "What is your average Dollar Per Lead (DPL)?"

Most of the time business owners do not have answers to these questions. Some can make educated guesses and come close, but is a ballpark guess how you want to run your business? We can't fault the business owner for what they don't know. We just have to give them the opportunity to learn processes that will help them.

When we first started Closer Secrets, we would talk to a variety of clients: some established companies, some new start-up businesses who had, at least, a base knowledge of how to track their business. Most of these clients had a customer relationship management system (CRM) set up, a scheduling system set up etc but they did not know how to leverage them to get a true picture of their profit and loss by lead type, by offer or by closer.

There is no doubt that a CRM is needed in your business. CRM's are a type of lead tracking that will help you build your client's profile. The optimal solution is customizing the CRM to mirror the optimal sales process flow and use Closer Secrets Lead Tracker to quantify the impact of each lead.

There is so much lost opportunity if you are not keeping detailed numbers. The true "meat" in a High Ticket Sales business is the ability to dive into the numbers. It will help you know where to improve your business.

Have a tracking system for your profit/loss, and the ability to pick out the high performing closers on your staff. Find the regions that are performing the best for your ad spend and focus more attention in these areas. This will provide you the key metrics you need to help you make bold decisions and truly move the needle for your business.

# Chapter 11: Winning Based on Fact Not Emotion

## Resolving Leads

Knowing the resolution to your leads is the backbone of a successful sales operation. One of the most important parts of a lead tracker is being able to quantify the resolution of your leads in detail. There is nothing more frustrating than doing a lot of work to realize you were mowing the wrong yard. It's the details that have us calling back the correct demographic of your leads.

Resolution tracking will come after the initial scheduled call with the client. Over the years we have broken down the responses we have received from our clients, and been able to categorize them into nine compartments. These nine resolutions will then be able to assist us in organizing the follow up sequence, that gives us the best opportunity to convert the prospect into a sale. Implementation of proper lead tracking and resolution codes means your sales team has the data to customize their approach with each prospect. These resolutions will help your business target the prospects with more qualified potential. Each resolution will have a recommended action from the closer.

It's important now to take the time to go over each resolution and the meanings and actions for each.

**Bad Number.** Nobody likes getting these types of leads, but they happen. The closer dials the number and all they get is the annoying buzz at the other end. Bad numbers are the leads that pop up where bad information was provided by the prospect. These are leads and data that we don't want our closers wasting time or business resources on. We want these categorized so they don't get thrown back into someone's lead pile, or looped back into the system.

**No Show.** These are the leads that took the time to book a call, but did not show up for their appointment. We realize that life happens, and that oftentimes, with the proper follow up, these leads can be contacted and converted into a sale. In this situation, the expectation we set with the closers is to call the prospect back a minimum of 3 times before the lead is marked as an official "No Show". Once that has occurred, the "No Show" leads will be targeted with a follow up email or text sequence that fits the acumen of the offer. We offer them a link to reschedule the call. We also will keep them in a profile that will allow for future contact for any promos or new products we have to offer.

**Canceled.** The resolution of "Canceled" is where the customer notifies us in advance that they will not be able to make the scheduled time slot. Typically this occurs over the scheduling link. Cancelled leads can be routed through a sequence attempting to reschedule. This resolution will also put them on the list for notifications for any new products or events that your company might produce in the future.

**Not Interested.** Sometimes, no matter how good your sales script, closer, or product, you will run into people who are just not interested in being your customer. They might lack money, time, motivation, or flat out misunderstood why they were scheduling a call. In this case we mark these leads as "Not Interested". This will direct our follow up sequence to re-target them when we have specific promos and new products. Just because they are not interested now does not mean they won't be interested in the future.

**No Money.** We are not out to make anyone feel bad about the situation they are in. We are ultimately looking to better the lives of those we come into contact with. The value of your business will come with an investment. However, no matter how clear that may be in your pre-call resources, not everyone will be in the position to invest. When a prospect has no capital, credit, or loan options, we disposition the lead as "No Money".

**Appointment.** When closers talk to prospective clients it's not always a "one call and done" situation. While some sales are done in one call, there are times that we need to let the situation breathe, not force the sale, and contact the lead within a specified amount of time. Typically, this will be due to the client being interested and needing/wanting to talk to a spouse or business partner, or needing some time to complete financial transactions in order to get the resources to invest into your program. In this case, we mark the lead as "Appointment". This would mean that there is a scheduled time and date to reconvene on a call and complete the transaction.

**Pending.** "Pending" resolutions are given to those leads that have a longer timeline than those that we would mark as "Appointment". These are the people who have told us they are interested,

## Chapter 11: Winning Based on Fact Not Emotion

and deemed qualified by the closer but might need a little time to get their ducks in a row. This timeline would be further out on the horizon with no specific set date for a call back. We mark these as "Pending" so they don't fall off the radar, and the closer remembers to circle back around with them.

**Payment Plan.** Congrats! The customer is in and has agreed to be a part of your program, but can not commit to the full financial investment at this time. This is where we make them with a "Payment Plan" resolution. We track the client this way so we know to follow up for any installments that are needed to bring them to paid in full. Once they are paid in full, we will change the resolution accordingly.

**Paid in full.** This means the client has agreed to be a part of your program/product, and was able to pay the full amount in one payment. There is no other action needed from the closer, other than to mark the resolution and guide the client to your customer success team for fulfillment. However, resolution does not mean that this is the last contact with your lead. With the resolution of "Paid in Full" or "Won" in the CRM, it is important to keep these clients in the loop for any promotional deals, upcoming events or new products your company might be releasing anytime in the future.

It is important to never forget about your previous customers when growing your business. Previous customers can be your most loyal ones. We recently had a client who decided to put on a live event and they wanted our closers to take the calls and/or dial leads for this event. The client ran a one-week promotion to kick off the sale of the event. Of course they did the ads and webinar and typical avenues to advertise the event. On top of this, we asked our client to provide a list of any previous buyers, to provide upsell opportunities for our team of closers. Closers sent out text messages to the list of previous clients to see if we could expand on the sales. At the end of the week promotion, we ran the numbers, and of the total sales for the company's live event promotion, 16% came from the previous buyers. That means of the 250 tickets sold to the live event in that week, 40 of them were from previous customers! At $3,000.00 a seat, that came to $120,000.00 of new profit brought in from existing, happy customers.

Resolution codes are key to keeping your follow up sequences organized and on point for your closers. When you integrate the proper resolution into your CRM it will help with time management for your closers and create a better user experience for your audience. Proper organization and data analytics will only benefit your bottom line.

## Geographic Ad Spend ROI

You created great ad content and purchased the space on your ad platform of choice, now what? If profit/loss numbers aren't getting you to the black, or generating the profit you were expecting, what are your options?

As a business owner, what information would you be looking for to help optimize your target audience? Are you thinking search engine optimization? Maybe you need to ramp up the language, or key words on your ads to hit your target market. What about knowing the effective target audience? Yes, these are all good things to think about, but it doesn't stop there.

Have you stopped to think that what you need to look at is the regions? Truly dig into the numbers that are coming from specific geographic locations that you are targeting. What regions are converting? More importantly, which regions are you spending your money on that bring little to no engagement? Are there regions where you are consistently getting dead end leads that are wasting precious resources your business can be using elsewhere? How can you find the profitable regions and avoid the others?

Closer Secrets was hired by a company to help elevate their business to the next level. The initial discussions were about updating web pages, getting an indoctrination sequence going, adding closers, refreshing their business menu, add this here, add that there, etc. These were all things that needed to get done to brand their business and bring excitement to their potential customers. They were spending money and working to get the value of their business out to the masses. Great, right? More ads means more eyes on your product. More people who see the value in your service. But here is the thing, sometimes the answer isn't more, it's less.

Sometimes it's the regions where you are targeting. Saving the

## Chapter 11: Winning Based on Fact Not Emotion

company's money by eliminating demographics that just don't convert. So how do you know which regions are not converting well? This is the another advantage of using a lead tracker, along with the CRM. The tracker will be able to provide data that you can pull, spin and compare on a multitude of levels. We can really get into the nitty gritty of not just how the leads are resolving, but where they are converting the best geographically. We can pinpoint what regions are working and which ones are wasting the company's time and resources. Having accurate numbers at your disposal quickly allows confident business decisions to be made at a steady pace. Think of all the time saved from milling around, compiling data and double checking. You can now confidently make real time decisions.

With one of our clients we put this plan into action. They were struggling with data analysis regarding ad spend. After using our strategies in a case study for about a month, we were able to take the data from the lead tracker and tell them exactly where they should stop targeting their ads. After reviewing the data with the customer they changed some of their targeting habits. Their dollar per lead (DPL) jumped from $200 per lead to about $350 per lead just by reallocating where they spent the money; wow! See what simple data analysis can do?

## Understanding your Numbers

We've said it before and we'll say it again, understand your numbers! Pay attention to the details, because the details matter. With this type of lead tracking system there is a plethora of data to collect. Not only the overall performance of the company but the broken down, week to week performance as well. We can target how the changes implemented affected the conversion of the deals. Did that new ad really work? Did the promotion do its job? Did cutting out that region change our profit margin? Was it human error? Perhaps the closer didn't do something effectively? Innovating and analyzing is crucial to making adjustments to increase overall profitability.

Randall Grizzle & Deborah Burris

# Profitability by Closer

When we meet with clients, we take the time to review their processes with general review and questions. What does their funnel look like? What is on their business menu? What do they feel is working for their business? Where are their pain points? What price points are converting for their niche? What is their ad spend? We gain pockets of information to help transform their business. Then we dig into a crucial piece of any business,

> "How are your Closers?"

A business can have the best products or services in the world, but if they don't have closers that convert sales it doesn't mean anything. Finding a top notch, world-class closer is like finding a pot of gold.

Most companies will know who their top producer is because it's the person getting the biggest commission checks. But do they know who is number two? What about the bottom two or three closers? Where's the gap in the race? Are they in a tight grouping of numbers? Or is there a huge differential between your top producer(s) and the rest of the pack?

The best way to reward your top performers is to position them for continued success. Put the top closers (those with the highest DPL, volume, and/or conversions) as a priority in the scheduling system. You want your top performers working your best leads. This will keep them motivated with nice commissions, and benefit your bottom line.

# Chapter 12: Motivating Compensation Models

*"People who succeed have momentum. The more they succeed, the more they want to succeed, and the more they find a way to succeed."*

-Tony Robbins

Sales people are motivated by two things: money and recognition. Having an attractive compensation plan for your offer feeds these two top motivations and will go a long way towards optimizing sales performance and bottom line results.

## Spiffs

Spiffs are used to create excitement and healthy competition amongst the sales team. A spiff is a chance to win extra cash or a prize above and beyond normal compensation. An example of a cash spiff is a $500 bonus for the sales team member that closes the most total volume for the week. An example of a prize spiff is a weekend for two at a resort. One of our favorite cash spiffs is a $500 cash bonus for the top setter for the week and a $500 cash bonus for the top closer for the week (in volume). In some cases, we have had one sales team member absolutely work their leads to the fullest and win both the setter and closer spiff. An extra $1,000 in anyone's pocket for one week's effort is sure to bring excitement!

Spiffs are a great way to get to know and engage with your team. We found that one of our teams had a large number of barbeque enthusiasts, so a Traeger grill was used as incentive. It ended up that one of our closers located in the Southern states won the Traeger! Spiffs like this continue to inspire not only the winner, but the other team members, as they watch him post the photos of his delicious barbeque creations on his social media page. They are all looking forward to that next Traeger spiff so they can show off their cooking skills; or their eating skills! The bottom line is that spiffs are fun! They light a fire under the entire team and feed the desire to be recognized.

## Static

The static compensation model gives a flat rate commission regardless of volume sold or dollar per lead (DPL) produced. This model is a good fit for new offers that have established a baseline for conversion.

As a general rule, lower ticket offers require a higher percentage commission to attract quality sales talent. Higher ticket offers can attract quality talent even if paying a slightly lower rate. The typical range for static commissions ranges from 20% to 40% of the gross sale.

## Sliding Scale

Sliding scale compensation is best suited for established offers with a track record of offer performance. With this model compensation is measured by two criteria:

1. Total Sales Volume and 2. Dollar Per Lead (DPL). A two-tier example of a sliding scale based on weekly payouts would be:

> Tier 1: Commission rate of 15% for DPL less than or equal to $500 and total volume of $10,000.

> Tier 2: Commission rate of 20% for DPL greater than $500 and total volume $10,000 +

## Chapter 12: Motivating Compensation Models

This model incentivises team members to treat every lead like gold, and follow up diligently to maximize each lead's potential.

## Payday: How and When

"Show me the money!!" Be very clear about when you will pay your sales team for each sales period. Typically, sales teams are paid for sales made two weeks prior to the current pay period to account for any refunds.

Sales professionals talk about money, collect money, and think about the money they anticipate hitting their account every moment of the day. The best way to shake off a bad sales cycle or be motivated to set a new personal goal is to reset and have a fresh start weekly.

Paying your sales team weekly can be a little more administrative work, but pays big dividends in mindset and motivation. If you cannot pay your sales team weekly, stick to a bi-weekly payment cadence at minimum.

# Conclusion:

At Closer Secrets, we have adopted 4 words as our guiding compass when determining who we work with. The acronym for these four words is G.I.V.E. which stands for: Gratitude, Integrity, Value and Energy. By staying true to this G.I.V.E. Mindset, we have drastically reduced closer turnover on the teams we manage. Business owners we represent have seen an average increase of 200% in their dollar per lead (DPL) while working with us.

## Gratitude

Gratitude is the state of being grateful. According to the Harvard Medical School, it is a "thankful appreciation for what an individual receives, whether tangible or intangible."

When the business owner expresses sincere gratitude for the role the closer plays in moving their business forward, and the Closer is truly grateful for the opportunity the business owner has provided for them to earn a livelihood, there is potential for a long-term sustainable and mutually beneficial relationship. If both parties do not operate from this place of gratitude, it does not matter how amazing the offer is, it will struggle.

> *Years ago I sold a high ticket offer for a team of key influencers. At first they worked well together and expressed gratitude for the strengths each team member brought to the business. They provided excellent training and professional development opportunities to the closing team. Everyone was energized, felt appreciated and financially prospered. Then, differences of opinion arose between the partnership, replacing gratitude with resentment. This spirit of thanklessness spilled over to the closing team resulting in a loss of sales and key closing talent. The offer was the same. The people were the same. The demand was the same. But gratitude was not present and the opportunity went from thriving to floundering.*
>
> *The number one key to a long-term, sustainable opportunity is gratitude. The business owner must remain grateful for his customer by excellent fulfillment.. They must also express gratitude for their sales team by acknowledging their contribution with enthusiasm and fair compensation. Closers must show gratitude for the opportunity by honoring each lead. After all, the business owner is the reason the opportunity exists.*
> *DB*

## Integrity

Integrity is the practice of being honest and having strong moral principles. It is simply: doing the right thing, especially when no one is watching. Integrity is a verb; it's something you do. It is a quality that is displayed by following through.

## Conclusion:

> *I have made it one of my most important traits with Closer Secrets that I will not lie, or mislead my sales teams. If things are good, I let them know. If the company is looking to make adjustments (lead sources, ads, team numbers), I let them know. I have been with companies where my sales lead leader was "Mr. Positive" ALL THE TIME. When the sales were good and the company was flourishing it was great to have those positive vibes flowing in the office. However, as you know, sales ebbs and flows. Sales teams know it, and when they recognize that there is a shift going on, (lack of leads, lack of sales, more meetings in the boss's office, team member's being let go, etc) and the team leader is still acting as if everything is great, it creates a lack of trust within the group. Yes, keeping morale high and staying positive is important, but never more important than the trust of your team. There is more respect and unity for the company when there is transparency.*
> 
> *RG*

Integrity is a non-negotiable. The business owners, sales reps, and everyone else in the company need to always come from a place of truth. When things are done the right way, there is much less to worry about.

## Value

Value is the importance, worth or usefulness of something.

Offering something to the marketplace that has the potential to change people's situations and make their lives better is truly a powerful position of responsibility. It is important that the Closers educate themselves so they can accurately communicate the value of the offer. It is essential that the business owner stands ready to deliver that value regardless of the customer's engagement or effort.

> *Over the years I have attended several new product launches, sales conferences, and self development seminars. One thing I found fascinating is how devoted some are to the community with which they align themselves. I was in a position of leadership at several of these gatherings. As a result, multiple people shared their experiences with me regarding their progress toward their goals and how they felt supported post-program purchase. The common denominator amongst all these experiences was the "value" the customer placed on the offer. Although they had not yet reached their financial goals with the program they purchased, their lives were better because they were on the path to the change they sought when they committed to their journey. Some of these individuals even felt so passionate about the value of the program, that they acted as ambassadors at the events, paying their own travel expenses to help others who were just starting out. All of this was possible because of the value these individuals perceived within the offer and community.*     DB

## Energy

Energy is the strength and vitality required for sustained physical or mental activity. In the simplest of definitions, it is the ability to do work. Civilization is possible because people have learned how to change energy from one form to another, including the energy from one person to another. Energy is contagious! It is displayed in the way we show up everyday. It is felt the second a person walks into a room or even picks up a phone.

## Conclusion:

> *Earlier I told you a bit about the opportunity I was offered to go to a Bio-hacking event. It was on the first day that I took away one of the biggest lessons from the week. Anthony was educating the group on Whim Hoff breathing. It's a technique of controlling your breathing by doing a series of short breaths and then holding your breath for thirty seconds. The idea is to push past the uncomfortable and see what you can really achieve.*
>
> *I was participating in the class, closing my eyes and taking the short breaths, and when it came to the long breath, I found myself holding it for around 18 seconds and took a "cheat breath". I opened my eyes to see everyone else with their eyes still closed, still holding their breaths. Anthony was leading the class and he noticed what I did. He looked at me and said "How you do this, is how you do everything." That hit me. It's the effort that I need to be putting in what I'm doing RIGHT NOW, in the moment. I have taken this lesson and now focus my energy on the present.*     *RG*

We are in control of the vibrations we put out. Make the decision to show up everyday as a person that you would want to be around.

Long term success is best achieved when your entire organization is aligned with key values, standardized processes, transparent communication and fact based decisions. Having a detailed "Playbook" for your business is the best way to clearly prepare, define and execute your game plan; ultimately setting you up for success for years to come!

### Randall Grizzle

Randall Grizzle is the founder and creator of Closer Secrets, a company designed to optimize business efficiencies and organize world class sales teams. With 15 years of experience selling for influencers himself, Randall saw the bigger picture on how to help businesses reach their potential. In 2017 Randall opted to stop selling for Russell Brunson (ClickFunnels) and go into business for himself. Randall and his team have made an impact on the sales community in just a few short years. Through his work ethic Randall has acquired clients who are authorities in the fast paced world of internet marketing. Closer Secrets has brought in over $20M in sales for their clients in 2020 alone.

Randall spent his formative years learning about hard work and grit growing up on a ranch, and earning a football scholarship to the College of Western Montana. While Randall is proud of his accomplishments, his most valued asset is his family. Randall is married to Valerie Grizzle. Together they are raising two children. It is a strong family value that is the backbone for Closer Secrets.

Deborah Burris

Deborah Burris has over 25 years experience in professional sales, team management and strategic business consulting. Her guiding philosophy is summarized by the word G.I.V.E, which stands for Gratitude, Integrity, Value and Energy. Consulting companies to incorporate these principles in their business has helped them improve key personnel retention and enjoy more sustainable success. As an entrepreneur launching several successful companies, these principles have been her compass to effectively balance her professional and personal relationships. In 2018, Deborah joined Closer Secrets as managing partner. Here she focuses on developing strategies and processes to help clients maximize profits and closers maximize performance.

Deborah has a Bachelor of Economics degree from Brigham Young University and a Master of Business Administration degree. She is a certified professional sales trainer and success coach, graduate of the Dale Carnegie program, former Assistant Director of the mentoring program for the National Association of Women Business Owners (NAWBO) and has been a speaker at Microsoft, NAWBO, and Infusionsoft/Keap. She is married to Christian Burris; together they have four children. Her highest priority and greatest joy is her family.

# Connect with Closer Secrets

https://closersecrets.com

https://www.facebook.com/groups/closersecrets

## Randall Grizzle

Instagram
@randallgrizzle.com

Clubhouse
@randallgrizzle

LinkedIn
www.linkedin.com/in/randall-grizzle

https://randallgrizzle.com

## Deborah Burris

Instagram
@deborahburris

Clubhouse
@deborahburris

LinkedIn
https://www.linkedin.com/in/deborahburris/

Facebook
https://www.facebook.com/deborahmburris

https://deborahburris.com

# → BONUS ←

Free BONUS ( $197 Value ) when you buy
The Ultimate Playbook for High Performing Sales Teams

What you get:
- Behind the Scenes Recording of : THE BIG PICTURE. ULTIMATE POSITION TO WIN & CRAFTING AN INTENTIONAL CULTURE
- The Importance of T.E.A.M. Hear from the Randall, Deborah and the High Ticket Closers from the world class Closer Secrets Team. Together they consistently sell six figures weekly, leading to tens of millions of dollars in sales for our clients.
- Learn what Closers *REALLY* want and value on a TEAM.
- Find out how in a competitive job, they have all learned to work together.

How to redeem your bonus :
1. Order Book
2. Go to https://closersecrets.com/bonus to receive your Free Bonus!

www.ingramcontent.com/pod-product-compliance
Lightning Source LLC
Chambersburg PA
CBHW070648220526
45466CB00001B/340